ANXIETY

IT HAPPENED TO ME

Series Editor: Arlene Hirschfelder

Books in the It Happened to Me series are designed for inquisitive teens digging for answers about social issues, certain illnesses, or lifestyle interests. These books feature up-to-date information, relatable teen views, and thoughtful suggestions to help you figure out stuff. Besides special boxes that highlight singular facts, each book is enhanced with the latest reading lists, websites, and other recommendations.

The following titles may also be of interest:

Activism: The Ultimate Teen Guide, by Kathlyn Gay
ADHD: The Ultimate Teen Guide, by John Aspromonte
Adopted: The Ultimate Teen Guide Revised Edition, by Suzanne Buckingham Slade
Autism Spectrum Disorder: The Ultimate Teen Guide, by Francis Tabone
Bigotry and Intolerance: The Ultimate Teen Guide, by Kathlyn Gay
Bullying: The Ultimate Teen Guide, by Mathangi Subramanian
College: The Ultimate Teen Guide, by Lisa Maxwell Arter
Creativity: The Ultimate Teen Guide, by Aryna Ryan
Depression: The Ultimate Teen Guide, by Tina P. Schwartz
Divorce: The Ultimate Teen Guide, by Kathlyn Gay
Eating Disorders: The Ultimate Teen Guide, by Jessica R. Greene
LGBTQ Families: The Ultimate Teen Guide, by Eva Apelqvist
Parental Death: The Ultimate Teen Guide, by Michelle Shreeve
Self-Injury: The Ultimate Teen Guide, by Judy Dodge Cummings
Sexual Assault: The Ultimate Teen Guide, by Olivia Ghafoerkhan
Sexual Decisions: The Ultimate Teen Guide Second Edition, by L. Kris Gowen
Shyness: The Ultimate Teen Guide, by Bernardo J. Carducci, PhD, and Lisa Kaiser
Siblings: The Ultimate Teen Guide, by Olivia Ghafoerkhan
Substance Abuse: The Ultimate Teen Guide, by Sheri Bestor

ANXIETY

THE ULTIMATE TEEN GUIDE

KATE FROMMER CIK

ROWMAN & LITTLEFIELD
Lanham • Boulder • New York • London

Published by Rowman & Littlefield
An imprint of The Rowman & Littlefield Publishing Group, Inc.
4501 Forbes Boulevard, Suite 200, Lanham, Maryland 20706
www.rowman.com

6 Tinworth Street, London, SE11 5AL, United Kingdom

British Library Cataloguing in Publication Information Available

Library of Congress Cataloging-in-Publication Data
Names: Cik, Kate Frommer, 1984– author.
Title: Anxiety : the ultimate teen guide / Kate Frommer Cik.
Description: Lanham : Rowman & Littlefield, [2020] | Series: It happened to me | Includes index. | Audience: Ages 13-18 | Summary: "Anxiety in teenagers is on the rise, and this book aims to help young adults cope with their struggles. Different types of anxiety, anxiety triggers, and coping strategies are accessibly explained, and personal stories from teens who have suffered from anxiety are included throughout to provide perspective and support for the young reader"— Provided by publisher.
Identifiers: LCCN 2019051362 (print) | LCCN 2019051363 (ebook) | ISBN 9781538121962 (cloth) | ISBN 9781538121979 (epub)
Subjects: LCSH: Anxiety in adolescence—Juvenile literature. | Anxiety disorders—Juvenile literature.
Classification: LCC BF724.3.A57 C54 2020 (print) | LCC BF724.3.A57 (ebook) | DDC 155.5/1246—dc23
LC record available at https://lccn.loc.gov/2019051362
LC ebook record available at https://lccn.loc.gov/2019051363

For Peretz

Contents

Introduction   ix

1   Overview of Anxiety   1

2   Why Is Everyone So Anxious?   21

3   Generalized Anxiety Disorder   37

4   Panic Disorder   55

5   Specific Phobias   71

6   Social Anxiety   85

7   More about Treatment—What Helps Anxiety   101

8   Comorbidity   125

9   For Parents   143

Conclusion   163

Notes   165

Further Reading   173

Index   177

About the Author   179

Introduction

Everyone experiences anxiety. That awful sense of impending doom, of dread, of heart-pounding panic is all too familiar, whether we've felt it in school, social situations, sports games, or moments of real danger. Those feelings are something that millions of people are struggling to manage on a daily basis.[1] As social worker Lisa Schwab put it, "If you are experiencing anxiety, you are normal."[2]

In every walk of life, we hear about anxiety. A recent study by the NCAA found that half of students reported experiencing high levels of anxiety.[3] Grammy-winning artist Adele—beloved for her soulful voice and touching music—has spoken of the horrible panic she feels before going on stage—panic that, at times, has led her to throw up or run out an emergency exit.[4] "My heart feels like it's going to explode because I never feel like I'm going to deliver, ever," she once said.[5] Jason Saltzman, CEO and founder of companies such as Alley and SeemlessDocs, suffers from generalized anxiety disorder.[6] Kylie Jenner and Nicole Kidman have a specific phobia of butterflies.[7] Ashley Benson, star of *Pretty Little Liars*, has spoken about experiencing frequent panic attacks so intense that she felt unable to drive or go to work.[8]

According to experts, anxiety specifically in teenagers is on the rise. In October 2017, the *New York Times Magazine* asked "Why Are More American Teenagers Than Ever Suffering from Severe Anxiety?" It was the most recent in a slew of articles (including "When Anxiety Hits at School" in the *Atlantic* and "Teen Depression and Anxiety: Why the Kids Are Not Alright" in *Time*) that discuss a steady increase in adolescent anxiety. In fact, data from recent studies claim that 31.9 percent of adolescents (ages thirteen to eighteen) have an anxiety disorder.[9] That is, at any given moment, almost a third of teenagers are experiencing symptoms consistent with these diagnoses.

If anxiety is so common, why do we feel so alone when we experience it? Why does it seem like everyone else is carefree while we struggle? Jason Saltzman noted of his experience, "I just thought it was all in my mind. I also felt insecure talking about it to anyone. It felt taboo."[10] Likewise Ashley Benson explained, "The person I was seeing at the time didn't understand, and my friends didn't understand, so there weren't people I could talk about it to. I felt crazy: Why am I feeling this way?"[11]

Many teenagers I speak with echo these same thoughts. They feel alone with and ashamed of their anxiety—like a tragic anomaly in a sea of happy, untroubled peers: "What's wrong with me?" "Nobody understands what it's like." "Why can't I cope, when everyone else does?"

Perhaps anxiety does not feel universal or "normal" because people experience it differently and in different situations. For some, staring at a complex math problem can bring on heart palpitations and constrained breathing; others would find that an enjoyable challenge. Some teenagers find social gatherings a good place to de-stress; for others, stepping into a party is paramount to jumping off a cliff with no net in sight. As one teenager, Iris, told me, "Yes, everyone experiences anxiety at some point in their life, so people will say, 'Oh it's really not that hard.' But everything that's simple for you is very challenging for me."

As a psychologist, I work with teenagers day in and day out, and what is most evident from speaking with them is that the pressure to keep it all together while suffering in silence is taking its toll. I cannot think of a better antidote than ending the silence and opening up those lines of communication: teens should hear from teens.

In an interview about the Student-Athlete Mental Health and Wellness Program at Wellesley College, Niki Rybko, the director of sports medicine and well-being, said, "The biggest thing is starting the conversation. . . . I think that colleges need to start putting on programming where starting the conversation is OK. Saying 'I have a mental health illness. I have anxiety. Some days I don't feel great.' That's OK." Rybko explained that her goal is for student-athletes to think about a mental health issue as they would any other injury. "An ankle sprain, you have to do your rehab, or else you're going to sprain it again. It's the same thing. If you're feeling low or are having lots of anxiety, you go get the help."[12]

This book is not a self-help book per se. Rather it is meant to share facts and information and personal stories—some of which you may relate to and some of which you may not. You will hear from young men and women who were happy to share their experiences because they hope to inspire and help you, just as others inspired them. There are lots of different parts to this book; you can skip to the ones that sound relevant to you. This book is simply meant to start the conversation.

OVERVIEW OF ANXIETY

What Is Anxiety?

Is it a feeling? A disorder? Your brain gone haywire? It's hard to categorize something that can feel like anything from a nagging doubt to a full-blown heart attack (and everything in between). Most people think of anxiety or stress as being a bad thing. "I need to de-stress" I hear people of all ages say. In fact, I'm pretty sure I say that too! A day with no work and no responsibilities? Yes, please!

The thing is, unlike some other mental health problems (like depression or hallucinations), which we'd be happy to completely eliminate, we need some amount of fear and anxiety for survival. Simply put, anxiety is your body's alarm system. It's pretty important that our bodies are wired to set off those fear alarms when we're walking down a dark street alone or our car starts to skid in the rain. That is scary stuff, and our anxiety protects us by sending us signals: "Get out of here! You're in danger! This could end badly!"

We even need some amount of anxiety in non-scary, everyday situations. Can you imagine if we felt no anxiety whatsoever? We would have no motivation. Study for that test so you can get a good grade? Nah, who cares. Surprise my friend with a great present for her birthday? Why bother. Listen to what your teacher said? Doesn't matter. Anxiety (when it is not running amok) is the kick in the pants we need to get moving and pay attention to the things we need to do.

This alarm system of ours can be broken down into several different components, which will likely sound familiar to you. There is an emotional component to anxiety—how you are *feeling* in the moment. There is a cognitive component—

> "'Are you sad? Do you get stressed? Do you have anxiety?' Yes, I have all those things, I'm alive!"—Ellen DeGeneres, Comedian, *Here and Now* HBO Special

Fizkes/istock via Getty Images

how you are *thinking* about and processing things. There is a behavioral component—what you are *doing*. And there is a physical (or physiological) component—what is happening in your body, as you're experiencing anxiety. For example, let's say you become incredibly anxious when your mom forces you to attend your family Christmas party. The emotional part of what you're experiencing may be fear ("Get me out of here!"), anger ("I hate my parents for bringing me here."), shame ("What's wrong with me?"), impatience ("Why are they taking so long to open presents?!"), or helplessness ("I can't handle this!"). The cognitive part of what you're experiencing may include worried thoughts or doomsday-like predictions ("What if everyone thinks I'm weird?" or "If I'm here for one more second, I'm just going to die!"). Our brains have a way of tricking us into interpreting situations in a negative, anxiety-inducing way. The behavioral component of what you're experiencing may involve crossing your arms, biting your nails, or hiding behind your brother. The physical component may include a racing heart, feeling queasy or lightheaded, or sweating profusely (even though it's December).

Of course, the cognitive, emotional, behavioral, and physical components of anxiety all interact, often feeding off one another in the most unhelpful ways. For example, as you settle into your desk in English class, you first have a thought, "What if my teacher hates the essay I just turned in?" This leads to some emotions, like anger ("I could have made it better if my parents didn't make me go to bed, stupid parents!") or shame ("I can't believe I didn't try harder on it!"). And then next thing you know, your body is responding as well (hands are sweating, stomach feels weird, and so on).

Sometimes it works in the other direction. Let's say you feel your heart starting to race as you're sitting in class. Before you know it, an accompanying thought pops into your head: "Why is my heart racing? I once read about a twelfth grader who had a heart attack. I might be having a heart attack! I can't take this for one more minute!" As you're thinking this, your emotions start to jump in—sheer terror!—and you grab your phone, stumble out of class, and send your parents an SOS text.

This second scenario—where an uncomfortable bodily sensation can make your anxiety spike—is a particularly common experience among people with anxiety (see "Intolerance of Anxiety" later in this chapter). Just as anxiety makes us misinterpret the world around us as dangerous (when it's not), it can make us misinterpret our own bodies as dangerous. Here's how psychologist Dr. Tamar E. Chansky summarizes anxiety:

$$\text{Overestimation of Threat} + \text{Underestimation of Ability to Cope} = \text{Anxious Response}^{[1]}$$

In other words, our brains magnify the danger while simultaneously convincing us that we're not capable of handling it, when in fact both these premises are completely false. How do our minds trick us like that? We'll talk more about that in a minute.

Where Does Anxiety Come From?

If you think about it, the only reason humans were able to survive for so many years was by having this built-in alarm system that alerted us to danger (thanks, evolution!). Long before there were AP tests to worry about, our ancestors had to be alert for things like vicious snowstorms and giant short-faced bears (yes, this was a thing). Like basically every animal that survived, we did so partially because we had an acute stress response, also known as a fight-or-flight response, that kicked in when we were in danger. (Those without this built-in response were probably dinner for a short-faced bear.) The fight-or-flight response is what your body does when faced with danger. To get technical, it's when your sympathetic nervous system discharges hormones, like adrenaline, into your body. This rush of adrenaline propels us to action. How do we escape this short-faced bear? Do we run or try to fight it? (Another lesser-known part of the response is to freeze, which is our body's fallback if we can't run or fight—basically play dead and hope for the best.) Today your anxiety may have different triggers, but that instinctual response is the same: sense of danger → adrenaline rush → fight, run, or freeze.

The way that you experience anxiety in your body is closely tied to this response. For example, your heart races when you're anxious. Why? Your sympathetic nervous system is making sure enough blood is pumping to your arms and legs so that you could run or fight if you needed to. Some people feel queasy or get a stomachache when they're anxious. Why? Your body is shutting down your digestive system so you won't have to think about food while you defend yourself from danger.[2]

It's important to note that this bodily response is not something you can *choose* to do or *choose* not to do. If you see that short-faced bear (or that airplane, or that crowd of gossiping juniors), and you sense danger, your body's natural instinct will take over and you will find your body doing *something*—running, freezing, fighting, heart pounding, sweating, or whatever it is—without ever having made the conscious decision to do it.

The Alarm System Run Amok

As we've established, some amount of anxiety is a good thing—it motivates us to work hard and it alerts us to something potentially bad happening so that we can be prepared. What psychologists Robert M. Yerkes and John D. Dodson found (over 100 years ago) was that there is an "optimal" level of stress for doing well. In their experiment, the "stress" factor was mild electric shocks given to rats. With moderate levels of shocks, the rats were able to learn and complete a maze faster. But with too little shocks or with more intense shocks, the rats did not perform as well.[3] The takeaway? Too little stress, and we don't do well at things ('cause . . . who cares?); we need some amount of stress to get energized and get the ball rolling. In fact, although it may sound strange, a little stress can even be enjoyable sometimes. Why else would we watch suspenseful TV shows, visit haunted houses, or willingly strap ourselves onto a four-hundred-foot roller coaster? When we're in the right mindset, some amount of heart-pounding anxiety can be downright thrilling!

However, when anxiety creeps past a certain level, it is no longer motivating or enjoyable. With too much stress, we can't focus, we're not good at problem solving, and our performance decreases. Like the rats in the experiment, when the stress is too high, we're left completely ineffectual. What we need to function well is something in the middle—a healthy amount of stress, but not so much that we get overwhelmed.

If you're reading this book, chances are that you are *not* at the optimal level of stress (and may have passed that point a long time ago). I'm guessing that

"Our brain is designed to protect us. It doesn't always know the difference between facing a hungry shark or saying hello to a stranger. It's up to us to teach it the difference."—Meera Lee Patel, author, *My Friend Fear*

you're at that far end of the curve, where anxiety is not acting as a helpful and motivating tool; it's causing you to feel trapped and unsuccessful. Our alarm system was meant to alert us to short-term danger, not to be blaring constantly, causing chronic stress. That rush of adrenaline was supposed to push us to run away from bears, not sit in our bloodstream day in and day out, making us worried about bears.[4]

When anxiety has become chronically overwhelming like that, it's not only *not* helpful in motivating us; it ruins the whole reason for having an alarm system in the first place. What's the point of an alarm system that is constantly alerting you to things that are *not actually dangerous*? Like a fire alarm that randomly rings at full volume for no reason, your system is not calibrated correctly. That tiny spider on your kitchen floor is not actually putting you in danger (nor are those gossiping kids in your class, for that matter), but your body is reacting as if it is. Going to gym class? *Anxiety*. Walking in the hallway? *Anxiety*. Sitting on a park bench? *Anxiety*. It feels like your body's alarm system is perpetually misfiring, leaving you paralyzed by fear and unable to do anything about it.

Irrational Thinking—How Anxiety Twists the Way We Think about Things

How do our misfiring alarm systems trick us into thinking things are dangerous when they're not? How do we end up feeling like saying hello to a stranger is as dangerous as a hungry shark? Simply put, our brains have sneaky ways of doing this; the technical term for these brain tricks is *cognitive distortions*. They are why we see the world as dangerous, when it's not. They are why you spent math class panicking about the noise outside that you heard earlier ("Was that a car crash? A gun shot?") rather than ignoring the noise and focusing on trigonometry (which, let's face it, requires your full brain power). These types of thinking patterns can turn a perfectly neutral experience ("That girl just glanced over at me") into a full-on anxious one ("She's judging me and will definitely talk to her friends about me so that no one will be friends with me"). Since everyone's brains play these tricks on them, it is important that you know about them. Here is a list of common cognitive distortions, in no particular order.

"I hate not knowing what's going to happen." *ozgurdonmaz/istock via Getty Images*

Intolerance of Uncertainty: "I Don't Know What's Going to Happen, and That's a Big Problem."

This is basically the crux of anxiety, isn't it? The world is uncertain and that stresses you out. Like most people, you like it when things are comfortable and predictable; knowing what to expect is reassuring. "Taking a new step, uttering a new word, is what [men] fear most," wrote Russian author Fyodor Dostoyevsky.[5] Most people thrive when their lives are (for the most part) routine, and they know how to handle the various parts of their day. It's called a "comfort zone" for a reason—that zone feels easy and manageable, basically the opposite feeling of anxiety.

Unfortunately, even without any major changes happening in your life, there are still a million unpredictable things that happen every day. "What will the weather be?" "Will my science test be hard?" "How will my friends react if I don't hang out with them after school?" "Will my teacher be disappointed if I don't do well on this assignment?" "Will my parents be mad or understanding about my bad grade?" There are endless unknowns.

Of course, life is uncertain for everyone, but that fact does not seem to bother most people. That is, many people are able to sit with uncertainty fairly comfortably. Sure, it may cause them to squirm or bite their nails once in a while, but it does not wreak havoc in their lives in quite the same way. They accept the unknown parts of life as unimportant—can't do anything about it, don't really care. Something unexpected happened? Roll with the punches. Or discuss it with your best friend on Snapchat 'til you feel better about it.

But for people with anxiety, these unanswerable questions or unpredictable events just add fuel to the fire. After all, a hallmark of anxiety is that feeling of helplessness, of being vulnerable to something dangerous. It follows naturally that anxious people would crave that feeling of predictability and control, in order to gain some relief from the feeling that things will end badly. You want your life to be knowable, foreseeable, and straightforward. You want to be absolutely *sure* that the situation is safe. Whichever uncertain, confusing area of life gives you anxiety (or maybe it's generalized, which basically means every area of life gives you anxiety) is like the thorn in your side. Your gut reaction will no doubt be to try to take charge of the uncertainty—to try to force it to be understandable and predictable (see the next section about control). Sadly, your struggle against this is 100 percent useless since life will always have a fair amount of uncertainty to it and there is not a whole lot you can do about that except learn to live with it. Easier said than done.

The Need for Control: "I Need to Get This Situation under Control Right Now."

Let's face it. We all love being in control of things. This is closely related to the fear of uncertainty that we just spoke about. When we don't know what's going to happen, we get nervous; when we're in control of what's going to happen (and therefore, we know with certainty what's going to happen), we feel good.

For people with anxiety, control feels *really* good (particularly since it's the antithesis of how they usually feel). At the root of anxiety is the feeling that you do not have control over whatever is making you anxious—your grades, your social life, an airplane, your health, even your own thoughts. I know many people with a fear of flying who say, "But I wouldn't be afraid if *I* were flying the plane." Being in control feels like the antidote to that pesky reality of uncertainty in life. You are the movie director, the principal, the air traffic controller. Nothing happens without your approval, and man, that feels great.

> "If I had one wish, it would be to be able to control my anxiety. Not get rid of it, but just be able to control it."—anonymous, age fifteen

I understand this mindset completely. When something anxiety-inducing happens, our first thought is usually to reassure ourselves that we are in control and not in danger. Someone you know got sick? "But that person doesn't exercise like I do," you say to yourself. Someone's house got burglarized? "But they live in a bad neighborhood and I don't," you explain. These thoughts are an attempt to combat anxious feelings by convincing ourselves that we have control over the situation and, therefore, are not at risk.

The problem is that just because you crave that feeling of control, it doesn't mean you can obtain it. Sure, it's great to exercise, but sometimes perfectly healthy people get sick. It's good to have an alarm system in your house, but even houses with alarm systems in nice neighborhoods get burglarized. The fact remains that the world is unpredictable and not always fair. And regrettably, no amount of planning, preparation, or mental gymnastics will change that. There's no way to control your English teacher's reaction to the essay you wrote, any more than you can control if a burglar will break into your house. This doesn't mean that you can't strive for order and predictability in your life (planning and routines are good, as are house alarm systems), but just keep in mind that the feeling of complete control over your environment that you crave will most likely continue to elude you. Professor of literature Joseph Campbell was quoted as saying, "We must be willing to get rid of the life we have planned, so as to have the life that is waiting for us."[6]

As an aside, I also want to mention that what feels like a normal amount of "taking control" to you may feel completely absurd and tyrannical to your friends or parents. People who don't understand anxiety may feel like you are just being stubborn when you insist that you cannot or will not do something that they think is perfectly reasonable (take a test, go to a party, call your grandmother on the phone, etc.). You can loan them this book to help them understand where you're coming from, but also keep in mind that they're not trying to take away your sense of control; they're trying to help you conquer the anxiety that feeds your need for control in the first place.

If reading the last few pages has completely discouraged you about ever feeling in control again, perhaps this idea will help: it's not the situation itself that is troublesome; it's how you're *thinking* about it. And (good news!), your own thoughts are something you *can* gain some control over (this is the premise of cognitive behavioral therapy, which we'll discuss in chapter 7). Anxious thoughts won't just go away, but over time, you can gain control over how much credence you give them. As Dr. Chansky says, "Just because worry has your number, and will try to talk your ear off, doesn't mean you have to listen."[7] If striving for control is one of the mental hang-ups causing you anxiety, see chapter 7 for more about how therapy can change the way you think about things—the world will stay the same, but you really will feel more in control.

Probability Overestimation: "Odds Are That This Is Going to Be a Big Problem."

Probability overestimation refers to the tendency to believe that bad things are more likely to happen than they actually are. For example, you might believe with absolute certainty that if you get on a plane, the odds of it crashing are high. Even though cruise ship accidents are extremely rare, you might have the distinct feeling that if you were to take a cruise, you would end up reenacting the *Titanic*. It's not that there's *no* chance of these things happening. Yes, in the history of the world, airplanes have crashed and boats have sunk, but the odds of it happening are extremely small. According to one source, the odds of dying in a plane crash are 1 in 5.4 million.[8] The odds of dying in a car crash on the way to catch the plane are actually higher than dying in a plane crash, yet fear of flying remains a common phobia.[9] As the *Economist* put it, "There is a special place in our psyches for the fear of big, unlikely catastrophes."[10]

In an effort to combat his wife's probability overestimation and fear of flying, a man named Nic Johns created an app for her (which is now used by thousands of people), called Am I Going Down?[11] The app calculates the odds of dying in a plane crash based on different factors like the airline that you're flying, the arrival time, the city you're flying from, and so on. After considering all these variables, the app gives you your chances: for example, for one flight from San Francisco to London on American Airlines, the app predicted, "If you took this flight every day, you'd expect (on average) to last 9,989 years before you went down." In other words, the odds are infinitesimal. You are *not* dying in a plane crash. And yet, I've heard anxious flyers say the odds of a crash are basically fifty-fifty. Or worse!

Probability overestimation could be a problem with any fear, not just flying. "When people struggle with fear they often have a hard time recalibrating their fear to the actual risk," explains psychologist David Tolin.[12] Instead of considering the facts of the situation (how many cruise ships do get into accidents?), we tend to become morbid fortune tellers, predicting and then believing that our own worst nightmares are going to happen imminently.

Mind Reading: "I Know What That Person Is Thinking about Me."

I'll be honest. I wish I were a mind reader. That would make me the best psychologist ever. Unfortunately, unless you're Professor X (founder of the X-Men) or a psychic, reading other people's minds is not something you can put on your résumé. Nonetheless, our brains sometimes trick us into thinking that we *do* know exactly what someone else is thinking. "I saw the way that girl looked at me.

"This is really, really bad." *Srdjanns74/istock via Getty Images*

She thinks I'm stupid." Or "My teacher didn't say 'good morning' when I walked in. He hates me." You don't have to have anxiety to have these kinds of thoughts, but anxiety certainly makes it worse. The fact of not knowing what other people are thinking is just excruciating (i.e., intolerance of uncertainty—see the earlier section), so we decide for ourselves what they are thinking. Unfortunately, mind reading tends to work only in the negative. I've never heard of someone thinking, "I saw the way that girl looked at me. She thinks I'm popular, beautiful, and amazing." Rather, the things that we "read" in other people's minds tend to mirror our own worst fears or ideas about ourselves.

Like most cognitive distortions, our brains become so confident about mind reading that we don't bother to evaluate how accurate these ideas might be. Could it be that your teacher didn't say good morning for another reason? Maybe because he was tired or had something else on his mind? No, your brain concludes that it's definitely because he hates you. Your brain has given you the gift of critical psychic powers—the worst superpower ever.

Catastrophizing: "This Is a Disaster!"

Catastrophizing is exactly what it sounds like: when things that shouldn't be a big deal feel like total catastrophes. It's making mountains out of molehills, as the saying goes. While most people would simply shrug something off, you are ready to declare a state of national emergency. Someone afraid of public speaking, for example, may find the idea of making a mistake completely devastating. Not just a little awkward. Not just a little cringe-y. Totally devastating! For someone with generalized anxiety, one bad grade on a test may feel like the end of the world. This is it; you didn't do well and now you're a failure forever! "In such states of mind, a minor injury is felt to be a mortal wound," explains psychologist Dr. Jennifer Kunst. "A difference of opinion is felt to be World War III."[13]

It's not uncommon to hear teenagers use this kind of catastrophizing language day to day: "If that happened to me, I would just die!" or "I'm totally going to fail this class." The thing is, most people don't really believe these things. Let's face it, most people just like being dramatic. For people with anxiety, though, the thought that their greatest fear will end in disaster is both real and terrifying.

Black-and-White Thinking: "It's Right, or It's Wrong."

This is a common way that people with anxiety tend to think about things. It's either right or wrong. It's either perfect or horrible. You're either a complete success or a total failure. There's no gray area. Why would someone feel the need to impose such a rigid structure on everything? Personally, I think it goes back to that whole control thing. The idea of the world being divided into strict categories and right or wrong answers is reassuring, if you are someone who worries about the unpredictability of life. It feels good to think that there's a "right" way to do things. (For this reason, I know many people with anxiety who much prefer subjects like math—that have clear-cut right answers—rather than subjects like English, which is more open-ended and subjective.) Unfortunately, most things in life are not black and white. Everyone has moments of success and moments of failure. But if the only two possibilities in your mind are perfect and horrible, and perfect is unattainable (who's perfect anyway?), you will end up feeling that most of what you do is in the horrible category. No matter how hard you try, it's never enough; it's never as good as you want it to be, so it must be bad. People like this are often as devastated by getting a B, as they would be by getting an F. If it's not an A, it's terrible.

Emotional Reasoning: "If I Feel This Way, It Must Be True."

"Trust your instincts" hails the Homeland Security website. "If it doesn't seem right, it probably isn't." This is the crux of emotional reasoning, in which we use our feelings as proof that whatever we are imagining is, in fact, reality. If I feel unsafe, it must mean I *am* unsafe. Many people swear by this idea. "Go with your gut" is a popular mantra that people often apply to relationships, job interviews, or just life in general. I'm not saying it can't be helpful; sometimes our gut feeling can make us aware of something that we knew from experience but couldn't explain consciously. (Malcolm Gladwell's book *Blink* gives countless fascinating examples about this.)[14] However, always trusting your feelings can be a slippery slope. Haven't you ever had an experience when you felt so strongly about something in the moment, only to completely reverse your opinion later? Maybe you were freaking out that you failed a test, but then you were thrilled when you got a good grade. Maybe you were furious with a friend because you thought she was ignoring you, but then you realized she was preoccupied with taking care of her new puppy. There are countless times when our feelings do not reflect the reality of our situation. They are just how we feel in that moment. Psychologist Dr. Avital Falk told me that she reminds her patients, "Thoughts are not facts. They are usually opinions or guesses."

If you're someone with anxiety, then many things in life give you an uneasy feeling or make you feel unsafe—it could be anything from the way no one commented on your Twitter status to that queasy feeling you got after eating lunch. But it does not mean that these things are *actually* problematic or unsafe, any more than freaking out that you failed a test is proof that you *did* fail that test. If you ask anyone with a fear of flying what their gut is telling them, they would say, "This plane will crash." Yet, as we just established, plane crashes are highly unlikely and that person *thinking* the plane will crash is certainly not going to *make* it crash. Bottom line, feelings can be misleading, especially if you are someone whose danger barometer is a little too sensitive to begin with. So, if you're looking to draw conclusions, best to look for lots of evidence, and not just rely on your spidey sense, no matter how accurate it feels.

Negative Filtering: "All the Negative Things I See Confirm What I'm Thinking."

Negative filtering is the cognitive distortion of choice for the pessimists or Debbie Downers of the world. That is, it involves only looking at the negative aspects of a situation, rather than taking in the positive and negative together as a whole. For example, you are giving a presentation in class and you see your classmate doodling; your brain zeroes in on it like a homing pigeon. "That's it. Everyone thinks this presentation is dumb and I'm dumb," you say to yourself. Never mind that everyone else in the class seems to be enjoying the presentation or that your teacher is smiling approvingly. Your brain brushes aside all that positive stuff and focuses exclusively on the negative things it can find to validate whatever depressing conclusion you've arrived at. (Notably, even if someone emphatically pointed

"I'm such a loser." *Khosrork/istock via Getty Images*

out the positive stuff to you, your mind would still find some reason to discount it: "If the teacher was smiling, she was probably thinking about something else. It didn't have to do with my presentation.") This kind of thinking can be particularly intolerable to friends and family, who may start to pull out their hair in frustration as they try to convince you to see the big picture.

I experienced this firsthand the other day when my husband and I were shopping at Costco, and he spent the entire time pointing out whatever negative things he could find—the avocados weren't ripe enough, they didn't have the kind of cereal he liked, the lines were too long (why had we come on a Sunday?), and so on. Later, back at home, as we were downing a giant package of delicious strawberries we'd gotten, he sighed and commented, "Should have gotten more of these. That was a mistake." By this point I had had it and gave him a long lecture about negative filtering, which he promised to keep in check. When you feel your thoughts headed in that direction, recognize that you are filtering the situation and try to reevaluate the evidence in front of you.

Labeling: "I'm a _____ [fill in the blank with an insult]."

Labeling occurs when you assign a label (either to yourself or someone else) based on some small amount of evidence. For example, you lose at a game of HQ Trivia and think to yourself, "I'm a loser." Or you knock over your water bottle and say, "I'm such a klutz." As with other cognitive distortions, you tend to ignore any evidence to the contrary (like that game of dodgeball you just *won* in gym class or all the times you *didn't* knock over your water bottle), and you quickly find a reason to discount it since it doesn't fit with the label you've decided on. Unfortunately, when you're anxious, the labels you assign yourself tend not to be flattering ones. (I never hear patients say, "I'm very popular" or "I happen to be an amazing athlete.") The problem with assigning labels is twofold. First, it makes you feel even worse about something that you didn't feel great about to begin with. No one enjoys losing a game, but if you see it as sealing your fate as a "loser," then that makes it even worse. Imagine for a minute that you lost the game and thought to yourself, "Oh well, everyone loses sometimes. Maybe next time I'll win!" That would put you in a completely different mindset. However, if you're determined to think of yourself as a loser, then the future does not look very promising. Why even bother playing games if you're a loser and will always lose?

Sometimes we label other people in equally unflattering ways. "She's a mean person," you conclude, after a girl in your class walks right past you without saying hello. It's true, she *might* be someone who's mean sometimes. That is one possibility. Or she might be shy. Or she might be thinking about her own stressful life. Or she might be tired and not in the mood to say hi. Or she might feel insecure about talking to someone she's not already friends with. The truth is, people are complicated, so there's no way that thinking about them as only one thing is accurate. Telling yourself that this girl is 100 percent a mean person is about as accurate as thinking of yourself as 100 percent a loser. And similarly to when we label ourselves, plopping labels on other people makes it more likely that we will rule them out entirely. I used to work with one girl who constantly complained that she had no friends at school, but when I suggested people who might be a good fit, she had a reason why she didn't want to be friends with each one. "She's annoying." "She's too quiet." "She's a goody two shoes." By labeling her classmates and refusing to see their positive *and* negative qualities, this girl had ruled out many potential friends.

Intolerance of Anxiety: "This Feeling Is Freaking Me Out!"

As mentioned earlier, an unfortunate aspect of having anxiety is that the experience of it can be triggering in and of itself. In other words, even if you're not thinking about the difficult math test or the stressful social situation, you may be freaked out just by the anxiety symptoms you are feeling: "My mind is racing and I can't stand it." "My heart is pounding and that's a sign that something is horribly wrong." "This anxiety is going to give me a stroke!" It is the feeling that the anxiety itself is unendurable, and something terrible will happen if it continues.

Sometimes, a little education about anxiety can help with this. Teenagers often feel some sense of relief knowing that the discomfort they feel when they become anxious is actually just discomfort, not a sign of something more. It may feel terrible in the moment, but it will pass and it certainly won't kill you. (For a great example of this, see Eliza's story in chapter 8.) "Healthy children do not have heart attacks because they become anxious or suffer collapses because of feeling afraid," confirm psychologists Dr. Eli Lebowitz and Dr. Chaim Omer.[15] If you can keep this idea in the back of your mind, it may help you to endure some of those feelings without starting to catastrophize. And having a solid understanding of how anxiety works, you may be better able to talk yourself down when you feel breathless or overwhelmed. When your brain jumps to "I can't stand this; it's going to kill me!" see if you can counter that thought with something like this: "You're just freaking out right now, it'll be okay." "This has happened before and everything turned out fine." "This is anxiety. This is *not* a heart attack."

Cognitive Distortions and Anxiety

The preceding cognitive distortions are just a few examples of how our brains trick us into feeling terribly about things, triggering unnecessary stress and anxiety. As you read through the list, I'm sure some sounded familiar, while others might not have. Often, it is easier to spot cognitive distortions in other people than in ourselves (which is why, as a therapist, I have an easier job than my clients). In our own minds, our thoughts seem perfectly reasonable and not unrealistic in the least. But taking a closer look at your anxious thoughts and reevaluating them for what they are—not facts, but distorted ways of thinking that cause anxiety—can go a long way toward being free of them. Dr. Tamar Chansky explains it as follows: "Just as we don't take copious notes on telemarketing calls, or pull out our highlighter pen when we're reading our junk mail—do we even read it?—recognizing that anxiety thoughts have little to offer us is half the battle."[16]

This book contains many personal stories of teenagers dealing with anxiety. In each case you could likely pick out the various cognitive distortions they have struggled with. For example, see Rachel's story on the next page.

Rachel's story is not that unusual; in fact, I've spoken with many teenagers who have had similar thought processes in high school. You may have had some of these same thoughts yourself! But now let's examine Rachel's thoughts with a critical eye to look for cognitive distortions. Catastrophizing? Check! For Rachel, a bad grade or a poor performance is not just a temporary setback. It is an all-out catastrophic disaster. Black-and-white thinking? Check! For Rachel, it is perfec-

Rachel's Story

If you had seen Rachel star in her school's full-scale musical theater production, you would never guess she had anxiety. When Rachel is on stage, she is confident, dynamic, and brilliant—a total rock star, and she's only fifteen! I was convinced she was ready for Broadway! Needless to say, I was surprised when Rachel's mother confided in me that she was struggling with some anxiety. Even Rachel's mother was confused. "She tells me she's really struggling, but I see a kid who is incredibly driven and focused and accomplished," her mother told me. "But I think she feels that [her anxiety] is constantly there and, at times, debilitating." From an outside perspective, Rachel is a straight A student, an accomplished actress, and the president of her class. On the inside, she feels constant pressure to succeed—to try harder and harder and accept nothing less than perfection.

When I spoke with Rachel, she confided that she has always been anxious, although it has gotten worse in high school. "I do a million different clubs and I take higher level classes and it's hard when you're doing all of that to not go crazy," explained Rachel. "I like my life, and that's why I'm so anxious about it. Because I want it to be good. Because I care about it."

Rachel's short list of goals for herself includes going to a top college, going to medical school, and becoming an ear, nose, and throat specialist. As a result, her grades are a persistent source of stress. "It's always like I want to be better, or do the best I can," explained Rachel. "If I get 100 as a grade, it means I did the best I could; there's no better than that. Getting a 100 means that I didn't have to try any harder. Look here: you did something that means you're perfect, 'cause it's the perfect grade. A 100 is just the most satisfying thing because it means you didn't do *anything* wrong."

When she scored a 3 on her first AP exam, Rachel was devastated. "A 3 is average, but I'm not an average person!" thought Rachel. "I don't know how this happened! In my head it's like, 'You have to work harder so you can do better.'" Rachel was both upset by her score and upset by what others would think of it. "How is everyone going to look at me now? I don't want to disappoint my teachers!" After receiving the score, she went to talk to her English teacher. "I said, 'I feel like I'm disappointing you,'" remembers Rachel, "and she said, 'You could never disappoint me!' But it barely registered."

On another occasion, Rachel got a C on a math test, because she had missed a key part of the directions. "I saw the grade and said, 'This is impossible! This has to be a mistake!'" remembers Rachel. When she looked over the test and saw her error, she started hysterically crying in the middle of the class. "I had such a breakdown 'cause I couldn't handle not being perfect," said Rachel. "I feel like everyone expects that from me . . . all of my friends. I'm supposed to be the smart friend! If I don't get the grades that I want, am I letting these people down?"

Any bad grade or social setback sent Rachel into a spiral of self-doubt. She had recurrent anxious thoughts such as "Could I have tried harder?" "Should I not have gone to rehearsal that day and studied more?" and "Should I cut these clubs out of my life so that I can have more time to study?"

"No!" she would argue back in her mind. "I like to do these things! They make me who I am!"

"But how am I supposed to do anything if I don't have good grades?" her anxiety would counter. "If I don't get good grades then I'm not going to be happy, and then I'm not going to be happy the rest of my life 'cause I'm not going to get into a good college."

Back and forth, Rachel would argue with herself. "It's really scary and it causes more anxiety, but then if I don't think about these things it's like, 'You're not thinking about your future enough!'" she explained. She felt caught in a vicious cycle of anxiety and self-doubt.

At times Rachel's thoughts became more negative, such as, "You're not good enough," "You're not smart enough," or "You'll never be successful." When this would happen, Rachel would start to feel her breathing constrict. "It's really scary," said Rachel, "I just always feel like I can't turn my brain off. . . . I want to go to a good college, and I feel like I need to get perfect grades and be the perfect student, and do all these extracurriculars and volunteer. . . . And I need to do all that while still staying healthy and having clear skin and exercising and doing all of these things and still being happy! I just feel like sometimes school is the first thing for me and I don't let all those other things happen."

"I just always feel like I can't turn my brain off." *recep-bg/E+ via Getty Images*

tion or nothing. Anything less than an A is a failure. No matter how hard she tried, it is not good enough if she made mistakes. Mind reading? Check! When she didn't do well on her test, Rachel assumed the teacher was disappointed in her (even when the teacher assured her she was not!), and she was convinced that her friends would feel she was letting them down if she didn't do well. In other words, Rachel's brain was presenting her with the most frightening or worrisome ideas—not the most realistic.

As you read about Rachel's cognitive distortions, did you start to think about your own? As with Rachel, your brain is tricking *you* into feeling overly worried or upset about things. And when that feeling of fear kicks in, your brain reacts the only way it knows how: fight or flight. "How can I stop this feeling/situation at all costs and escape the danger?" Remember, this is not your calm, rational brain thinking. This is your adrenaline-energized brain looking for a fight or a flight—a confrontation or an emergency exit. And most anxious people are not fighters, so that leaves the flight option. Sometimes this involves a literal flight (as in running out of the school building as fast as you can), but often, it is a more subtle escape: hiding in the bathroom during math class, wearing headphones or looking intently at your phone to avoid talking to people, or avoiding stress-inducing activities altogether. Either way, you are fleeing from whatever set off those danger alarms.

What do *you* do, when your anxiety level creeps up? Where does your escape instinct take you? Many people scoff when I ask this and justify the ways in which they avoid things that make them anxious. "It's not a problem," they might say. "I just don't like talking to people." Or "Who uses trigonometry in their life anyway?" To be honest, these excuses are just *another* way of avoiding the anxiety which is causing issues in your life in the first place. Whatever kind of anxiety you have, avoidance is most certainly a part of it (see chapter 5), which will need to be addressed.

Conclusion

To sum up, anxiety is a totally natural and normal human response—our body's alarm system—without which, we would have been evolutionary toast. But like anything, you can have too much of a good thing, which then becomes not such a good thing. When our alarm systems become *too* sensitive, alerting us to danger when there is none, it can wreak havoc on our ability to function. We instinctively go to great lengths to avoid the things that feel unsafe, although paradoxically, this avoidance makes us feel even more fearful and unsafe.

At the heart of anxiety is often distorted ways of thinking about and evaluating situations—making decisions based on faulty premises. Unfortunately, our brains are telling us that these ideas are not faulty—they are facts that you should pay attention to and worry about. Once our brains have successfully convinced us, our bodies follow by avoiding the situations that we've decided are dangerous.

Think about the ways in which your brain persuades you that you should be anxious. Talk through your greatest fears and then see if you can spot the cognitive distortions. It isn't easy (that's what therapists are for), but understanding the way anxiety works is an important step in getting a handle on it.

WHY IS EVERYONE SO ANXIOUS?

In the world of research, the jury is still out on whether rates of anxiety among teenagers are, in fact, increasing, or whether we have just gotten better at identifying it. (Whereas previous generations had more of a suck-it-up-and-deal attitude toward mental health issues, we've come a long way in realizing how important these issues are.) At the very least, research has shown that teenagers today are reporting being less and less satisfied with their lives and are seeking out mental health treatment more than ever before.[1] Anecdotally, many mental health professionals, parents, and even teenagers themselves reported to me that they do see a strong increase in adolescent anxiety. Why is that? What is making teenagers more anxious? There is not a lot of solid research out there yet,

pixelfit/E+ via Getty Images

but here are some interesting theories that are worth considering—see if any of them ring true to you.

Academic Mania

As our world gets more and more fast paced, so does our education system. If you talk to your grandparents about what it was like for them going to school, I guarantee you will hear something that sounds very different from what we're used to today. In fact, many people of that generation never made it to high school, let alone college. Leaving school to work in the family business or get a different job or even join the navy used to be much more commonplace fifty years ago. But in today's world, where preschool increasingly looks like kindergarten and kindergarten increasingly looks like first grade, the pressure to reach academic benchmarks earlier and earlier is intense. According to a recent survey from the Pew Research Center, academics was the top stressor identified by teenagers.[2]

"There's so much pressure in the schooling system," explained one girl I spoke with, who is currently a sophomore at a public high school. "Everything is taught toward the test. Nothing is just learning for learning anymore and I think that puts a lot of pressure on people." She added, "And why are we still using an education system that's not even relevant to us? There's no room to be creative or be a really deep thinker in school anymore."

For many teenagers, the pressure to get through each day of school, slogging through classes that don't make sense to them and will never be relevant to their lives, is an incredible stressor. For others, it is the pressure to get into a good college. According to one study, in 1940 only 5.5 percent of men and 3.8 percent of women were graduating from a four-year college; by 2017, six times more men (33.7 percent) and nine times more women (34.6 percent) were doing so. Simply put, there are many more college applicants now. The competition has intensified.

"I think adolescents are under a level of pressure that at least when I was growing up, I wasn't under," psychologist Dr. Jacqueline Ferraro, who has been treating teenagers for almost forty years, told me. "To be so accomplished academically, to get tremendous grades so you can go to the right college, the SATs, the ACTs, these tests that determine so much of their lives. . . . And I think parents put a lot of pressure too. All their hopes and dreams get put on the adolescent. To go to the best school, to have this particular future and income and success, so parents can feel like they've done a good job parenting because their child is a success." It seems that, for some families, the days when it was okay to have grades that were average or "good enough" (but not "outstanding") are long gone; whether this pressure is coming from parents or internally, from adolescents themselves, it can result in an incredible amount of anxiety.

Notably, this pressure seems to affect both teenagers who are academically inclined and those who are not. That is, if you're bad at reading, you're stressed because you're constantly being forced to read. But even if you're good at reading, you may *still* be stressed, because you feel the pressure to achieve even more; since you're good at reading, you *should* be getting an A (see Rachel's story in chapter 1). Is school one of your top stressors?

Screen Time: 1
Friendship: 0

How much time do you think you spend on electronic devices? Two hours a day? Four hours a day? More? Of course, not all of that time is fun and games (and social media); much of that time may be spent doing homework assignments, adding things to your calendar, checking emails, or performing other mundane tasks that just happen to be on electronic devices these days (when was the last time you saw someone use a paper calendar?). I was surprised when my iPhone automatically started telling me how many hours per week I was logging on my phone—it was definitely a higher number than I would have thought.

Psychologist Dr. Jean Twenge has researched all kinds of patterns of different generations of teenagers. Her most recent book, *iGen* (short for the Internet Generation), describes the patterns of your generation (i.e., current teenagers and young adults), and according to her research, teens are spending nearly all their leisure time on electronic devices—going online, texting, using social media, gaming, watching TV, and so on. (I have to say, this surprised me less after I saw the crazy amount of time that *I* was spending on my phone each day; I'm far from being a teenager but those things are addictive!).

As Dr. Twenge notes, this time spent on screens has to come from somewhere. So, if teenagers are spending more time online, what are they doing less of? According to the research, teenagers today are spending less and less time with their friends *in person*—on average, an hour a day less than teenagers spent with their friends in previous generations. As unstructured activities like hanging out at the mall get replaced with structured activities like piano lessons, the bulk of teenagers' social lives may be happening electronically. "For iGen'ers," writes Twenge, "online friendship has replaced offline friendship."[3]

"Is that such a bad thing?" you might wonder. In some ways, social media has allowed us to expand our social circles—to keep in touch with camp friends or cousins across the world and strengthen relationships that would not have been possible a generation ago. In theory, these technologies are about connecting people, but the research seems to show that they have the opposite effect: making teens feel more isolated and worse about themselves and their friendships.

"For iGen'ers," writes psychologist Jean Twenge, "online friendship has replaced offline friendship." *tommaso79/istock via Getty Images*

According to Twenge's research, teenagers who spend more time on screens are more likely to feel lonely, depressed, and even suicidal. (By the way, this is also true of adults, whose Facebook use was directly linked to feelings of unhappiness.) In contrast, those who spend more time with their friends in person are significantly less likely to be unhappy, worried, lonely, and so on. "If you were going to give advice for a happy life based on this . . . it would be straightforward: put down the phone, turn off the computer or iPad and do something—anything—that does not involve a screen," writes Twenge. "Compared to a warm person right in front of you, electronic communication is a pale shadow."[4] Or as one of my favorite Internet quotes puts it, "Do more things that make you forget to check your phone" (source unknown).

More Screen Time, More Anxiety

OK, so teens are spending more time online and less with their friends. Why would that cause more anxiety? Researchers have a few hypotheses about this connection. First, it has to do with social media. Think about Instagram, Twitter, Facebook. You post something and then you wait for the likes. Likes mean that people approve of you—that they think you're attractive or cool or popular. If you do get a lot of likes or positive comments, you feel great. But if you don't get a lot of likes? Or if your friend's picture gets more likes? Or if some of your friends are tagged in a picture that you're not tagged in? Enter anxiety and self-doubt. Meanwhile, scrolling through other people's pictures and posts does nothing to alleviate that anxiety, since you start to notice that everyone else looks beautiful, popular, and exceedingly happy. Why don't you feel that way? Is there something wrong with you?

Since you can access social media *all the time*, it can become a constant stressor. In this way it is different from other kinds of social worries. Let's say you are anxious around your classmates at school. "Are they really my friends?" you think. "Was what I said weird?" "Do they think I'm a loser?" "Do they think I'm fat?" At least with school, there is a final bell that will ring, after which you can get a nice afternoon/evening break from the pressures of your social life. But with social media, there is no break. The Snapchat messages and group texts can go on into the night and will be waiting for you when you wake up in the morning. "When I was at my low," explained one young adult I spoke with, "seeing people on Facebook or Instagram going out, laughing, and having fun brought me down even more. Cause it's like, I don't have anyone to do this with. . . . I want to be doing this, but I can't."

Now let's say we add another complicating factor: people being mean. What if the social issues are not all in your head? What if someone posts a nasty comment about you or deletes you from the group chat? Unfortunately, using social media to bully others—whether it's saying mean things, making threats, posting embarrassing pictures or videos of someone, starting rumors, or excluding others—is extremely common; one study reported that in 2016, 34 percent of students experienced cyberbullying.[5] Like communication in general, bullying using technology is just easier. It does not involve saying things to a person's face and it can be done anonymously, from the safety of someone's own bedroom. Many people who write comments like "You're ugly," "No one likes you," or "Go die" wouldn't dream of saying that to someone's face, and yet posting online seems to bring out the uninhibited worst in people. "Social media are also the perfect medium for the verbal aggression favored by girls," write authors Greg Lukianoff and Jonathan Haidt. "Social media gives middle and high school girls a 24/7 platform to carry out the verbal aggression they favor, ostracizing and excluding other girls."[6] (Boys can be cyberbullied too, although research shows that teen girls are most affected perhaps because, on average, they use social media more often.)[7] It is no surprise that teenagers are reporting feeling increasingly lonely and left out. In sum, the combination of more social stress (online) with less social support (in person) can make teens' anxiety skyrocket.

People often use social media as a platform for bullying. *Artist: Chana Rosa Bogart*

Communication Has Changed

"One of the biggest ways to manage anxiety is to be able to *talk* and work through problems," psychologist Dr. Jessica Welt told me. Hence the reason why talking is the basis of most kinds of therapy. The more you talk about it, the less scary it is. (And if you've never experienced an all-out, teary, soul-bearing heart-to-heart conversation with a friend, parent, or sibling, you really should try it. It feels fantastic!) But with the interjection of social media in our lives, technology has changed the way we "talk." Think about how many of your recent conversations with friends were in person, and how many were on text, or WhatsApp, or Snapchat, or Twitter. As we grow accustomed to that kind of online "talking," it can take a toll both on our social skills and our ability to manage our anxiety.

But hasn't technology made communication easier? Yes and no. Like the idea that social media allows us to be more social (which we just saw is not exactly true), communicating via technology is not necessarily all it's cracked up to be. I can't argue with the fact that it is easier to send a text to your friend, rather than starting a whole conversation on the phone. It's also easier to send an emoji than put into words what you are thinking or feeling. It's easier to chat with a "friend" in a chat group once in a while than with a friend who you see every day at school. But these things aren't serving quite the same purpose that good ol' face-to-face interactions do. We use the same terms to describe these communications—*talking, chatting,* and so on—but in fact, they are quite different. When we communicate face-to-face with people, we are constantly practicing and honing certain skills: how to start or carry on a conversation, how to joke around, how to read people's intentions (Are they mad? Are they kidding?), how to empathize with someone, how to resolve conflict, and so on. These interactions are what lay the groundwork for close relationships, and unfortunately there's just no substitute for them. As Dr. Twenge explains it, "An hour a day less spent with friends is an hour a day less spent building social skills, negotiating relationships and navigating emotions."[8]

Research has actually shown that our brains are hardwired specifically for face-to-face social interaction. In the human brain, we have a collection of cells called "mirror neurons," which get activated both when we do something (smiling, raising our hands, and so on) and also when someone else does that same thing. That is, if you see someone smiling, your brain has *the exact same reaction* as if you yourself were the one smiling. Think about how infectious someone else's mood can be. A friend is sad, so you end up being sad; someone is happy, so you end up being happy. But it doesn't happen unless you actually *see* the person.

Have you noticed that moods just aren't as contagious via text message? I don't think this has been researched yet, but I'm pretty sure we don't experience any mirror neurons firing when we look at an emoji. In-person interaction is the basis for how we bond with each other and form relationships. If you think about human evolution, it makes sense that we would have developed strong social bonds because we stayed in close proximity to one another; we humans *had* to be social and stick together in hunter-gatherer times, because if you weren't part of the tribe, your chances of survival were not great. As Dr. Twenge puts it, "Being a hermit was literally bred out of us."[9]

Now think about conversations through technology. Gone are the burdens of normal conversation. You can start or stop a chat at any time and it's not awkward. Long periods of time can go by while you think of something to respond. You don't need to say anything particularly interesting (I've seen whole "conversations" of just emojis). You can say things that might be kind of weird to say in person. And if it's getting uncomfortable for any reason, you can just close out the chat. No muss, no fuss.

Again, I can't argue that it's not an *easier*, more time-efficient way to communicate. Yet, rather than making our interactions simpler, it seems that these new avenues of communication are just making things more complicated. For example, it can be hard to read people's intentions in a text, and sometimes the emojis just make things more confusing. ("What did she mean by that poop emoji?") I frequently have middle school students in my office hurt and confused by something that happened on social media. "She said, 'You're so annoying' but she's supposed to be my best friend," one girl told me. I asked if she was kidding: "Did she mean that in a joking-around way? Or is she mad at you about something? Was it in the context of a fight? Or were you two teasing each other?" If the conversation was face-to-face, all these questions would be clearly answerable, but social media dulls our ability to interpret and manage social interactions with others.

I have experienced this firsthand. There have been several occasions when I had great online conversations with people I "met" online, after which I would think to myself, "I really like them. They're so easy to talk to. We should be friends!" However, I was sorely disappointed when I *did* meet them in person, realized we had no actual chemistry, and could barely carry on a conversation. Somehow, online communication is just not the same thing, and when we are fooled into thinking that it is, it makes our interactions with others all the more confusing and unsatisfying. Naturally, when teens are left second guessing these online communications and feeling insecure about their relationships with friends, it can cause their anxiety to increase. If talking and friendships are two of the major antidotes to anxiety, think about how social media use is undermining them both.

Exposure to Information

There is just too much information out there. The world has always been complicated and stressful (ask any history buff), but there was never a time in history when we had to hear about it 24/7. The invention of social media keeps us perpetually up to date on *everything*. Sometimes that's good. We can easily access news stories, learn more about politics, or keep tabs on our friends. The downside is, there's just no break. It's not like you have to catch the five o'clock news anymore. There is news *all the time*. And let's face it, most news is enough to give anyone a headache. Nuclear weapons in North Korea? Constant school shootings? Countless celebrities guilty of sexual misconduct? It's pretty disturbing. "I was watching the news the other day . . . brought to you by Paxil. Well now I need it!" joked Ellen DeGeneres, in a standup routine. "There should just be one [news]

INFORMATION OVERLOAD
Oksana Stepova/istock via Getty Images

crawl that goes around over and over again: 'Things are getting worse.' That's all we need."[10]

In 2018, *Time* ran an article titled "Is It Bad for You to Read the News Constantly?" Yes, was the author's opinion, based on the findings of a survey by the American Psychological Association. "More than half of Americans say the news causes them stress, and many report feeling anxiety, fatigue or sleep loss as a result," reported author Markham Heid. "Yet one in 10 adults checks the news every hour and fully 20% of Americans report 'constantly' monitoring their social media feeds—which often exposes them to the latest news headlines, whether they like it or not."[11] Another article, in the *Guardian*, compared news to sugary food in its toxicity; that is, it is fun to ingest, but it does not fill us up or nourish us in any way. "News is to the mind what sugar is to the body," suggests author Rolf Dobelli. "Unlike reading books and long magazine articles (which require thinking), we can swallow limitless quantities of news flashes, which are bright coloured candies for the mind."[12] In other words, although they look appealing and may be enjoyable or exciting in the moment, at the end of the day, they are doing us more harm than good.

Furthermore, unlike in years past, when you probably didn't hear about disturbing news items until you were older and appropriately mature (and/or paid attention to what your parents were talking about), kids of all ages are now exposed to pictures, messages, and videos with all kinds of violent, sexual, or disturbing content. "Gone are the days that you could protect your child from information that was emotionally more than they could handle developmentally," explains Dr. Welt. "There's so much more exposure to these kinds of things and kids don't have adequate resources to deal with them." Several other psychologists I spoke with echoed these sentiments and noted that they have had multiple cases of teens coming to therapy because they were disturbed by things they'd seen online—ISIS beheading people, sickening pornography—that they did not know how to handle.

Research has shown that people are much more likely to remember "emotionally charged" events than other, more mundane events.[13] This explains why you can't for the life of you remember those algebra formulas you learned (or even what you had for dinner last night), but you can replay in your mind every detail of the finale of *The Walking Dead*. If it scares or upsets us, we'll remember it. I know many teenagers (and adults) who are haunted by upsetting news items or video clips they saw online while they were clicking around news sites or social media postings.

Furthermore, research has found that our brains pay more attention to the gist of emotionally charged experiences than to the actual facts and details of the experience.[14] Evolutionarily, this makes perfect sense. Our cavemen brains didn't need to learn the details of what a woolly mammoth looked like or smelled like when it was attacking—we just needed to learn to get the !?$%# out of there! Life or death! The same is true when we see disturbing content online. Extending beyond the details of what we've seen, we're left with a lingering sense of upset that sticks in our memories. Things are bad. Life is scary. We may not even be able to trace these thoughts back to their original sources, but we are left feeling bothered by them nonetheless.

While staying informed is a good thing, the burden of filtering how much information is too much information is now on us, and it requires a good deal of boundaries and self-control. "I tell people who I work with to find some way of using media where they feel in charge of it—that the phone isn't with them twenty-four hours a day," psychotherapist Patricia Schell Kuhlman, LCSW, told me in an interview. "You have to, in some way, be your own captain of the ship—how am I going to steer through all this? What am I going to do?" If you are starting to feel overwhelmed by both the content and quantity of information coming your way, you may want to speak with a parent or therapist to come up with a good way to set limits for yourself.

There's No Roadmap

In every previous generation, we often looked to parents and grandparents to help us navigate tricky or confusing times. It was generally assumed that being an elder meant you had some life wisdom to offer, and once teenagers stopped rolling their eyes about it, they could really benefit from their parents' advice. The problem is, in today's world, your parents and grandparents have never experienced many of the stressors that you're dealing with. Most teenagers I know end up teaching their parents about technology, as opposed to the other way around. So how on earth could parents give you advice about cyberbullying? Or understand a Twitter fight? How often do you need them to really explain things if you could just google the answer yourself? As technology has sped up our world, it has left a big generational gap, which can leave both parents and teenagers feeling adrift.

Adolescence Is a Transition

Your teen years are naturally a time of transition—you are crossing the confusing and frankly disconcerting bridge from childhood into adulthood—and times of transition tend to raise our level of anxiety. Think about times of transition you've gone through in the past: going to sleepaway camp, starting a new school, being with a new group of kids you don't know. It's anxiety inducing. Now, add the complications of being a teenager to that transition. You are figuring out your social life, your sexuality, your body, your hopes, your dreams; in short, you are figuring out who you are. You're starting to realize that your parents don't have all the answers (although they still think they do).

This is not a new phenomenon like technology. Teenagers have been trying to figure this out (that is, figure *themselves* out) for as long as there have been teenagers. (Famous developmental psychologist Erik Erikson wrote that the essential challenge of adolescence was "the struggle for identity"; "identity confusion [is] obviously a normative and necessary experience.")[15] However, there seems to be a general consensus that all these "normal" pressures have significantly intensified of late. The pressure to be popular. The pressure to be attractive. The pressure to be good at everything: school, sports, playing an instrument, volunteering, being a leader—the list goes on. Even the pressure to "just be yourself" can feel like a stressor when you're not quite sure who you are yet. "One of the things that happens to adolescents is that they're told a lot of things about themselves: 'You're not working up to your potential' or 'You should be able to do this,'" Kuhlman told me. "So I'm always trying to help people tune into to their inner sense of themselves and see what makes them feel comfortable or uncomfortable." With all the pressures in today's world, the transition of adolescence and the task of figuring out who you are has become a great deal harder.

In addition to figuring out who you are, becoming an adult can come with a whole host of practical challenges. It's not just the big identity questions; it's the day-to-day nitty gritty stuff too. Interviewing for jobs or colleges, taking standardized tests, learning to drive (unless you're a city kid like I was), making your own decisions about your schedule, classes, extracurriculars, social life—these things make most people nervous, but for someone with anxiety (who craves predictability and feeling in control), any and all of these challenges may cause your mind to start racing and your palms to start sweating.

Labels, Labels, Labels

Although defining oneself has always been a part of teen life, many people I spoke with felt that the increased presence of social media forces teenagers to label themselves, even if they don't feel particularly confident that the label exactly fits. Are you straight or gay? Bisexual, pansexual, panromantic, or polyamorous? Do you identify as a man, a woman, or nonbinary? Where do you stand politically? Where do you stand on social issues?

There are a multitude of options and labels available to us—possibly more than ever before—but for some people, these labels only contribute to their uncertainty and their anxiety. For example, it can be disconcerting when you see children or teenagers even younger than you who seem to have clear answers to all these questions, and you feel like you don't yet. "I think it can be a pressure in a certain way to know who you are at a time when you're still exploring who you are," Kuhlman said. "In a traditional culture, you just have your role and you do it. Nowadays we don't have as many traditional roles. . . . In general, a climate that's friendly and supportive of whatever differences a child has is a good thing, but it can contribute to anxiety." In other words, we have more freedom to be whoever we want to be, but more pressure to figure out who that is, and figure it out soon.

For example, Kuhlman described a young man she treated who now identifies as nonbinary but in high school was not sure what he was. Though he was quite athletic, he found he could not relate to the other guys' talk of girls and sexual experiences. "Are you gay?" his teammates would ask him, and he would answer "I don't know," which was incredibly anxiety provoking. He felt the pressure to find the right label for himself but wasn't sure what that label was.

Similarly, I recently had a fifteen-year-old girl in my office who considers herself nonbinary and pansexual, but right now she has a crush on a boy, who also has a crush on her. "So does that mean I'm gay or straight?" she asked. "And what does that make him? It's very confusing!" It *is* confusing. It's supposed to be confusing. It's a hard thing to sit with, but it will make you less anxious if you keep in mind that you don't have to pick all the right labels for yourself right this minute. You don't have to have all the answers. Let a crush be a crush—no labels necessary. With any luck (and some soul searching and maybe even some therapy), it should all come into focus by adulthood.

A Culture of "Safety-ism"

Today we live in a time and place where mental health concerns are, for the most part, understood and respected. (If you're wondering how far we've come, read some accounts of how American society handled depression, anxiety, or posttraumatic stress disorder fifty years ago. Hint: not well.) And with that understanding, our society has shifted to a more respectful position on people's individual needs. For the most part, I'd say this is a great thing. As a psychologist, I love the fact that our society has become more psychologically aware and actually helps people get their needs met rather than brushing them aside.

So, what's the down side? Putting such an emphasis on "emotional safety" can be a double-edged sword. In an effort to make everyone feel comfortable, we sometimes fall into the trap of making too many accommodations—helping people to avoid risk or conflict at all cost. We adopt the mindset that if something makes you feel uncomfortable or unsafe (or emotionally unsafe), you should not have to do it. For example, Jeannie Suk Gerson, a professor at Harvard Law

School, wrote an article in the *New Yorker* about teaching rape law. Obviously, it is important that prospective lawyers understand the laws about rape, but professors are increasingly getting push back from students who find it too triggering to hear about, and demand that they be either given "trigger warnings" or that the "offensive" content be removed from the class entirely. "For at least some students, the classroom has become a potentially traumatic environment, and they have begun to anticipate the emotional injuries they could suffer or inflect in classroom conversation," wrote Gerson. "They are also more inclined to insist that teachers protect them from causing or experiencing discomfort."[16]

Although it is well-intentioned, helping students avoid topics they find triggering (or even just potentially upsetting) is most certainly counterproductive (see chapter 5 for more on why safety behaviors do not help anxiety, but rather feed and prolong it). As authors Greg Kukianoff and Jonathan Haidt summarize it, "Avoiding triggers is a *symptom* of PTSD, not a treatment for it."[17] The same could be said for all kinds of anxiety. The more you try to control your environment and avoid stressors, the less prepared you will be to handle and grow from them.

Your goal cannot be to feel safe and comfortable all the time. If this is your current goal, or your parents' goal for you, it needs to be reevaluated. Your goal should be to feel strong, resilient, and capable of tackling whatever curveballs life throws at you. To be in a position where you are able not only to handle them but to learn and grow from them. Ever heard the phrase "What doesn't kill you makes you stronger"? (This was originally attributed to philosopher Friedrich Nietzsche, but you might be more familiar with the Kelly Clarkson version.) Another variation of it is "No pain, no gain" (which started out as an exercise motto, but really can be applied to a lot of things in life). The idea is not just that you managed to survive difficult situations; it's that you are actually better off because of them. Think of when you were a baby, learning how to walk. In order to learn that skill, you had to practice over and over again, falling on your face every step of the way. You may have sustained a few bruises, but you came out with a whole new skill. (Can you imagine if your parents had carried you everywhere as a baby so that you never fell down or got hurt?) The same is true of many things in life—the harder you try, the more times you fall, the more there is to gain from the experience. In contrast, if we never tried new or challenging things, two things would happen. First, we would not get to grow, have new experiences, or feel a sense of accomplishment. Second, we would not develop any tolerance for struggle or hard work or even for being out of our comfort zones. Without strengthening those muscles, any small challenge we came across would feel mountainous and overwhelming. Think of the quote "Without rain, nothing grows. Learn to embrace the storms in your life" (author unknown). Without embracing new challenges head-on, we miss the opportunity to grow and learn from them.

Author and academic researcher Nassim Nicholas Taleb explains the concept in the following way. According to Taleb, people are not fragile; they are *antifragile*. That is, they are the opposite of fragile. Not only are we *not harmed* by stressors; we actually thrive when exposed to risk and randomness. This may sound absurd to you, a person with anxiety who is trying their hardest to avoid risk or stressors at all cost. But if you think back to a time when you worked hard to accomplish something stressful (whether it was passing a test, training for a sports team, learning to play a musical instrument, etc.), you will recall that that glow of accomplishment afterward feels pretty darn good. Certainly it's a "high" you would not have experienced if you hadn't pushed yourself. "Wind extinguishes a candle and energizes fire," Taleb explains. "Likewise with randomness, uncertainty, chaos: you want to use them, not hide from them. You want to be the fire and wish for the wind."[18]

Conclusion

Although the research is inconclusive, widespread anecdotal evidence and the number of people seeking mental health treatment suggest that anxiety rates really are increasing among teenagers and young adults. The million-dollar question is, why? There are a number of possibilities, some of which are new to our society (e.g., social media) and some of which are not so new (e.g., the uncertainty of transitioning to adulthood). As you read through these descriptions, which ones rang true to you? Are you a social media addict? Do you not spend a lot of face-to-face time with friends? Do you feel like you don't have good supports (parents, grandparents, peers, etc.) who can guide you and give you advice in tough situations? Do you feel the pressure to find the right label to define yourself? Are you incredibly stressed about reaching milestones like getting your driver's license or your first job? It is most likely a combination of a lot of things, but identifying some of the factors that may be contributing to your anxiety can help you figure out the next steps toward getting a handle on it.

GENERALIZED ANXIETY DISORDER

··

Now that we've covered the basics of anxiety and some pretty common patterns of anxious thinking, in this chapter we will discuss generalized anxiety disorder, or GAD. You will hear some facts about the definition, read about symptoms and treatment of GAD, and hear from three amazing teenagers who were kind enough to share their stories. If GAD is something you've been diagnosed with, or if you have a sneaking suspicion it might apply to you because you're super anxious, read on.

Definition and Symptoms

According to the fifth edition of the *Diagnostic and Statistical Manual of Mental Disorders (DSM-5)*, generalized anxiety disorder is defined as "excessive anxiety and worry" that lasts more than six months, about a number of events

Other Physical Symptoms

- Heart palpitations
- Shortness of breath
- Feeling lightheaded or dizzy
- Sweating, chills
- Nausea or feeling sick
- Vomiting
- Blurred vision[a]

Other Emotional Symptoms

- Feeling nervous, tense, wound up
- Feeling frightened, fearful, terrified
- Being edgy, jumpy, jittery
- Being impatient, frustrated[b]

or activities.[1] Symptoms can include restlessness, fatigue, difficulty concentrating, irritability, and sleep problems. To be diagnosable, the person must find it "difficult to control the worry" and the symptoms must be severe enough to interfere with a person's functioning.

The definition makes the criteria for GAD seem clear cut, but whether your anxiety qualifies as "excessive" can be hard to figure out. One teenager told me that she was puzzled when her pediatrician recommended that she see a therapist for anxiety, because she thought she had just been chitchatting about the very *normal* drama in her social life.

So, when is anxiety normal and when is it severe enough to be considered "a disorder"? Basically, what the *DSM-5* definition tells us is that someone with GAD has had a lot of different worries for a long time, and the worries are so bad that they are making it hard for the person to get through the day. The individual may not have any different fears than anyone else, but they find themselves overrun with worry most of the time. Think of Piglet from *Winnie the Pooh*. Although surrounded by friends who care about him, he is generally stuttering and panicked with various worries. Moreover, the worries get in the way of him doing fun things and generally going about his life. When Pooh and Tigger encourage him to come camping with them, he replies, "I don't know. . . . My house might miss me." And on another occasion, "No, I'm not coming out. It's too dangerous for such very small animals."[2] Luckily, Piglet's life mostly involves things like ice skating with the gang or looking after Rabbit's garden, but for teenagers today, there are a lot more stressors lying in wait to spike their anxiety.

As the "generalized" part of the disorder name suggests, worries and fears are not necessarily related to something specific (like a fear of flying or spiders, or in Piglet's case, Heffalumps). Rather, it could be any number of things—often in combination with one another. Fears about health: "What if I get sick?" "What if my dad gets cancer?" "Am I crazy?" Fears about friends: "What if my friend gets mad at me and won't talk to me anymore?" "What if all my friends are talking about me when I'm not there?" Fears about school: "What if I'm late

"Haunted by Anxiety." *Artist: Rebecka Grunberg*

to class?" "What if I fail the test?" Fears about family: "What if my parents get divorced?" These are just a few categories, but there are countless others—appearance, physical safety, the future. Any topic is fair game for anxious thoughts! Sometimes these worries can come in the form of questions (the "What if" types of questions, like those mentioned) and sometimes they can be stated as facts: "If I go to school today, I know I'm going to feel sick." "If my boyfriend sees me upset, he'll worry about me." "If I get sick at the party, it will ruin everything." Often the focus of the worry hops around from one topic to another, even as the overarching cloud of anxiety stays the same.[3]

The confusing part about these worries is that many of them may be valid, making it difficult to tease out what is in fact a thought that warrants anxiety and what is not. Some fears are somewhat realistic (if not all that likely), whereas others may be wild conjecture, but it can be hard to tell which is which. Equally confusing, there are many times when it is hard to pinpoint a reason for the worry at all. "I have this unsettled feeling and I don't know why." "Something's not right." "I'm going to screw something up." As one teenager put it, "It's being anxious all the time and you don't even know what the fear is. It's completely irrational." Another girl I spoke with explained, "I just wake up feeling like I want to cry, and I don't know why."

What Causes GAD?

- *Genetics*. Blame the parents. Like all anxiety disorders, there is a genetic component to GAD, meaning that if you are experiencing it, it likely came from somewhere else in your family. Ask your parents about other family members (grandparents, aunts, uncles) who you suspect may have similar struggles.
- *Gender*. It's true! Girls are more likely to have GAD than boys are.
- *Temperament*. That is, your personality. Some people get angry under stress, some people get sad—you get anxious (or all of the above).

Hayley's Story

When I met Hayley, she was a bubbly, smiling, adorable fourteen-year-old. Everyone loved her—boys, girls, adults, and teachers. So, when she first told me about her anxiety, I was surprised. She could have fooled me. In fact, she was fooling just about everyone, but keeping up the facade was taking its toll. "I like being perfect," Hayley admitted. "People would say 'you're always so happy and you're always smiling.' It was almost like a drug. Those little things—you become addicted to hearing them. . . . And you get nervous because without it—if someone thinks of you differently—you don't know what to think of yourself anymore."

The pressure to maintain her "perfect" persona was extremely emotionally taxing. Hayley's anxiety began to spike—her legs would shake, she would become nauseous and vomit, and she started pulling out her hair. "I couldn't tell people when I was upset or when I was mad at them and that would drive me insane," explained Hayley. "I just didn't want to tell people how I was actually feeling 'cause I wanted to appear differently."

After a while, Hayley's nausea was so bad that eating at all became physically unappealing, and she felt hungry less and less. She was anxious all the time but could not pinpoint a particular fear. In an effort to maintain her good grades, she would stay up late and wake up early, causing extreme physical exhaustion. Hayley tried a slew of medications, none of which helped to calm the anxiety. By ninth grade, Hayley felt like something was very wrong with her. She would often cry uncontrollably and have trouble breathing. Just getting out of bed became a battle. "I wasn't happy being me, but I didn't want to be a fake person," Hayley explained. "People would say, 'why can't you just be yourself?' I *was* being myself, but I didn't like it. . . . It all made me feel nuts."

Kieran's Story

Kieran, age fifteen, remembers being anxious as far back as third grade, but she wasn't diagnosed with generalized anxiety disorder (along with major depressive disorder) until ninth grade. For Kieran, it was the constant nagging feeling that she was an outsider—the "odd man out." While from the outside it seemed like she had lots of good friends, on the inside she became increasingly anxious. She compared herself incessantly to others. "I'd sit down next to someone and compare our leg sizes," Kieran explained to me. "I'd think, I'm that much bigger than everyone else and no one will like me because of it."

The more she compared, the more worried she became of how others were viewing her. Convinced that they were thinking negatively about her, Kieran would ruminate on her every interaction. "I doubted everything I said," she reported. "I remember things I've said years ago—things no one else would remember! Like I said 'hi,' but it wasn't at the right moment maybe, so I'd contemplate it for a really long time." The summer before ninth grade, Kieran was prescribed Zoloft to help with her anxiety and depressive thoughts. However, it had the opposite effect, causing her anxious and depressive thoughts to worsen. Kieran's anxiety became so bad, that she refused to go to school to avoid the panic that it triggered—the feeling that she couldn't breathe and a pounding in her head. She would go to sleep at 7 p.m., wake up at 10 a.m. and still feel exhausted. "I *wanted* to go to school," Kieran said. "Even in the depths of the darkness, it was always a dream to go to school and get good grades, but I just couldn't."

Chelsea's Story

It wasn't until she started high school that Chelsea started to feel intensely anxious. The youngest of three, Chelsea had watched her older brother and sister cruise through high school and had seen her dad's disappointment after each of their parent-teacher conferences and the awkward family discussions that followed. A few weeks before she started ninth grade, her father came to talk to her. "I know he didn't mean to put pressure on me," Chelsea told me, "but he said I was his last chance. . . . I saw how my sister and brother went through high school—they didn't really try. I thought if I don't try as hard as I can now, I have no future. And that was kind of my mindset when I got to high school. I have to work extra hard now because 'future me' would be really mad at 'past me' if I didn't. I don't want to let anyone down. That's one of my biggest fears, letting people down."

Although she didn't show it, Chelsea felt constant anxiety about her grades: "A 95 was never good enough. An A– was never good enough. People would tell me 'B+ is an amazing grade for this class' but I would still stress myself out!" Chelsea began spending her lunch periods meeting with teachers, to make sure that she would not fall behind. "I know every single inch of the teacher's office by the end of the school year, I'm in there so often," joked Chelsea.

When she became anxious, Chelsea would fiddle with her fingers and her legs would start to shake uncontrollably. "When my breathing gets really heavy," explained Chelsea, "I know there's something wrong. . . . I'd get this feeling. It felt like all my insides were being squeezed out into a two-inch jar and I couldn't breathe."

At times, Chelsea's anxiety seemed predictable; for example, she knew it would spike before a test. But increasingly, her anxiety became unpredictable, spiking without warning when she was with friends or just walking down the hall. "It all started with academics and needing to be the best in the class and then it took over my life," explained Chelsea. In an effort to focus exclusively on schoolwork, Chelsea deleted all her social media accounts, as well as her Netflix subscription—a way to guarantee that there would be no distractions. Though she had always considered herself a social person, she began to feel increasingly isolated from her friends. "It's hard cause you show up to school the next day and you hear 'Oh my god, did you see what she posted?' Or 'Did you get that Snapchat?'" explained Chelsea.

> No, I didn't. . . . In a way I get a boost up cause while you're spending ten minutes on Snapchat, I'm spending those ten minutes studying for that test we have tomorrow. So, on the one hand, I feel more confident. On the other hand, I feel like I'm missing out on four years of my life. People look back on this and remember the times they spent with their friends and I'm looking back and remembering the 100 percent I got on the math test. . . . But I want to have as many opportunities as I possibly can. I don't want to limit myself if I'm just hanging out with friends.

The more isolated Chelsea became, the more awkward she felt in social situations. Although she appeared the same on the outside—smiling, happy—on the inside, she became increasingly unsure of herself and her friendships. "In eighth grade I would have talked to everyone and asked how their day was. I did it with ease!" recalled Chelsea. "And now what's in my head is 'I know they don't like me.' That's really the first thing I think of! 'No one likes me in this room so how can I work my way up from here?'"

As a result, Chelsea's anxiety would often spike in social situations and she would have to excuse herself to go for a walk, or listen to music to calm down. "Oh my god, I hate myself" became her catchphrase. "It's one of those things teenagers say but the more you say it, the more you start believing it," said Chelsea. "And I do, at a certain point. . . . I think, what's there to like?"

The more Chelsea doubted and criticized herself, the more sensitive she became to her interactions with other people, and her anxious thoughts would often lead to that familiar feeling of lightheadedness and tightness in her chest. If someone wasn't looking at her directly, did they really want to be talking to her right now, or were they just pretending to be interested? If Chelsea said something that she hadn't fully thought through, would people think she was stupid? If a friend teased her that nobody liked her, was there some truth behind his joke? If someone sat down to talk to her, Chelsea would immediately think, "Do they feel bad for me?"

"It's a completely distorted way of thinking!" exclaimed Chelsea. "I hope no one else thinks like this!" Then she added, "It's the worst when people say, 'So just don't think about it.' I hear myself and I know it's stupid, but I'm going to keep stressing about it. . . . My sister and my mom told me I had to see a therapist and that scared me even more because I don't have time for the other thousand things I have to do. I never really put my mental health first."

"It's the worst when people say, 'So just don't think about it.'" *diego_cervo/istock via Getty Images*

Treatment: Getting Help

As we learned in chapter 1, some amount of anxiety is both important and necessary to our functioning. If we had zero anxiety, we'd probably never learn or accomplish anything! We'd perpetually not care, not try, and not get those fantastic feelings of self-accomplishment when we succeed. At the same time, if we have too much anxiety, we can't learn or accomplish anything either. Therefore, the goal of GAD treatment is not to get rid of *all* anxiety. The goal is to reduce your anxiety until it is not as intense, not as overwhelming, and just much more manageable, so that you can get on with your life. It's one thing to worry about a test you have coming up so that you're motivated to study. It's another to be reduced to tears every morning because you can't stop thinking about a bad grade you got three years ago. Being anxious all the time sucks up a lot of energy—it's exhausting! What a relief to have that energy available for other things.

Because it is a slippery slope from feeling appropriately anxious about your life, to feeling like you are going crazy because you can't stop worrying about things, it can be hard to identify when exactly anxiety becomes a problem. Unlike a panic disorder, it can be hard to pinpoint a distinct moment when generalized anxiety starts and even harder to determine when it has become excessive. But chances are, if you are reading this book, your anxiety may be reaching unmanageable levels, so let's talk about what can help.

It is important to keep in mind that what helps and resonates with one person may not necessarily help or resonate with another. Just as the experience of anxiety is very individual, so too is the treatment of anxiety. As you'll see, Hayley, Kieran, and Chelsea all found very different sorts of things helpful in treating their anxiety. There is no one-size-fits-all way to "fix" generalized anxiety, but here are the most common kinds of treatment:

- Medication
- Therapy
- Mindfulness
- Self-help books
- Other strategies

Medication

For treating generalized anxiety disorder, psychiatrists tend to recommend some kind of anti-depressant medication, such as an SSRI (selective serotonin reuptake inhibitor) or an SNRI (serotonin-norepinephrine reuptake inhibitor; see chapter 7 for more info on both of these). Psychiatrist Dr. Simon Epstein told me that he has found Zoloft and Prozac to be the two most effective for teenagers. If those don't sit right, his third choice would be Wellbutrin. "Zoloft and Prozac have had the most research for treating adolescents and the results are good," he said. These medications also come in liquid form, in case swallowing pills is not your thing.

The downside? It takes at least two weeks for each medication to take effect, which means that you could be waiting awhile to get some relief. In addition, it can be somewhat of a guessing game as to which medication will be the right fit

Side Effects of Medication

- All medications have potential side effects, and everyone's body can react differently. It is important to discuss these side effects with the doctor who is prescribing the medication.
- Side effects may include
  - weight gain
  - dry mouth
  - nausea or diarrhea
  - insomnia
  - dizziness
  - sexual problems
  - feeling nervous or agitated

for each person, so there may be some trial and error (and side effects) before you find the right medication. "There may be side effects," Dr. Epstein acknowledged. "I don't have a crystal ball either . . . , but those are things we're going to talk about every week to make sure we don't have that problem."

Therapy

For teenagers with GAD, most doctors will recommend that they attend some kind of therapy, in addition to any medication they may take. Even if medication is helping to reduce the anxiety, therapy can get to the bottom of where some of those anxious thoughts and feelings are coming from in the first place, and teach you ways to deal with them. Psychologist Dr. David Andersen explains it like this: "Anxiety is maintained because you're ruminating, and you can't stop thinking about something again and again and again. Ruminating is an attempt at thinking your way out of having a feeling, and it doesn't work. What does work is letting yourself have the feeling." This may sound terrifying but facing the anxiety and naming those anxious thoughts is what actually helps you get past it. Psychiatrist Dr. Dan Siegel puts it another way: "Name it to tame it!" Another catchy aphorism: "Feel it to heal it!" That is what therapists are there to help with.[4]

Hayley's Story, Part 2: The Treatment That Worked

Although she had been in individual therapy for several years, read several self-help books that didn't help, and tried countless medications, Hayley's anxiety continued to worsen throughout high school. "In my head it was like, 'I can't live like this,'" said Hayley. "I needed to be able to get better."

It wasn't until she participated in a day treatment program (a program with therapeutic services several times per week) the summer after her junior year, that Hayley started to feel a sense of hope. "With individual therapy, you can feel alone in it," explained Hayley. "Having a group of people who are going through the same thing was really helpful. It's a very individual process but it's helpful to go through an individual journey together." Seeing other people overcome their symptoms inspired Hayley to feel that she could do the same.

Therapists who led the groups encouraged the participants to voice their thoughts and fears and then taught them strategies for how to cope. As Hayley described it, "When you're learning how to do it, you have to go through all these negative thoughts—naming all the worst things in the world. I came home every day crying! But then you learn how to deal with them. It's hard to jump in, but you have to."

In the group, Hayley learned to differentiate the "anxious voice" in her head from the "rational voice." She began to keep a journal—often writing out conversations between the two conflicting voices. This allowed her to take a step back from her thoughts, observe them a bit more objectively, and notice when she was thinking irrationally and jumping to the worst possible conclusion. Worrying that she's a burden on her friends: irrational. Worrying about her teenage cousin who uses drugs: rational. In addition, the therapist encouraged the group participants to think of alternate responses they could have to an anxiety-inducing situation, and then think through how these different responses could affect the outcome differently. It proved a helpful exercise to Hayley, giving her mind alternate ways to look at a situation that was making her feel trapped.

Now in her senior year of high school, Hayley acknowledges that she is still anxious, but she feels much more in control of her anxiety. "Most days I'm at least 80 percent in control," she estimates, "I have a ways to go, but I can deal with it." And when she does have anxious thoughts pop up—"What if no college accepts me?" "Wherever I end up going, I'll be miserable"—she is able to use the skills she learned to label those negative thoughts and recognize them as irrational. In addition to the things she learned in therapy, Hayley has a slew of other coping strategies at her fingertips for when she feels her anxiety start to rise—stretching, baking, doodling, and listening to music often do the trick, but Hayley still finds journaling to be the most helpful. "[Anxiety] is something that you have to deal with, but it's important that you're not defined by your anxiety," Hayley concluded. "It shouldn't be your identity."

What research has shown is that pretty much all therapy is effective (that is, better than no therapy) and that no one kind of therapy is radically more effective than any other.[5] Therapy can happen in groups or one-on-one. Therapists may use a structured approach (for example, having you fill out worksheets, set goals for each session, and so on) or a more hands-off approach, in which they listen to the things you talk about and discuss them. Either way, the idea is to help you get a good understanding of where the anxiety is coming from, face those feelings, and learn how to cope with them. Think of Dr. Anne Sullivan on *Pretty Little Liars* or Dr. Sharon Finkel on *The Flash*—even superheroes need therapy!

There are many different kinds of therapy (many of which have catchy acronyms), but for GAD, the two most common kinds of therapy that you're likely to hear about are cognitive behavioral therapy and psychodynamic therapy. For more details about what these are and how they work, see chapter 7.

The downside to therapy? Unlike medication (which will likely have some effect on your body whether you want it to or not), therapy requires some amount of buy-in from the patient. If you're not willing to show up for sessions, open up to the therapist, and give it your all, then there is probably not much a therapist can do for you (we're not magicians!). It's like that joke about therapists: How many therapists does it take to change a lightbulb? One, but the lightbulb has to *want* to change. Dr. Frank Lawlis summarizes the idea like this: "Whenever you make a conscious decision that progress will not or cannot be made, you will always be proven right."[6] In other words, if you're convinced that therapy is a waste of time, chances are, it will be.

Kieran's Story, Part 2: The Treatment That Worked

When Kieran's anxiety and depression reached their peak, her mother took her to an inpatient hospital, where she stayed for two weeks. There she started different medications and felt calmer being in a new, stable environment. When she returned home, she began going to individual therapy twice a week. Although skeptical at first, she gradually felt more comfortable with the therapist and started to open up. She remembers the therapist using the metaphor of a lily pad to describe life: a lily pad has to be balanced and if one side is weighted down by something, it throws everything off. Finding balance would be the key!

When Kieran tried deep breathing and meditation, it didn't work for her ("Meditation just makes my brain race," Kieran explained), so her therapist encouraged her to try strenuous physical exercise—"to exhaust her body to the point that her mind couldn't keep up." Kieran joined her school hockey team and immediately fell in love with the sport. "It really does relieve stress," reported Kieran. "The endorphins of exercise really help me. I went to every practice [this season] including the 5 a.m. practice, which was so hard to get up out of bed for." As a hockey novice, the season was full of challenges for Kieran and several times she was on the verge of tears. She would think to herself, "I'm done. I don't want to do this anymore," but would find the strength to push past the discomfort and finish each exercise. The feeling that she really *could* do it was exciting, and Kieran started to feel proud of herself.

Now that hockey season is over for the year, Kieran has started to feel a dip in her emotional state, but she continues to see her therapist and has reached out to some of her hockey teammates to schedule some practices. It has been a year and half since Kieran's stay in the hospital, and she feels much more in control of her anxiety, although she continues to struggle with self-doubt. "When I'm with friends, I don't doubt our relationship . . . but at home, when I'm by myself, I start to think about what could go wrong. 'Do they actually like me?' I do have moments where I doubt," acknowledged Kieran, "but it's not the constant it used to be . . . it's not at the forefront of my head at every minute." And when the worry creeps up again? Kieran knows that physical exercises help her—whether it's something small like cracking her knuckles or sucking on a lollipop, or something strenuous like hockey. She also loves reading, journaling, doing art projects, and writing poetry when she feels anxious, and she takes time to remind herself of a helpful mantra—that she can always make a fresh start. "I tell myself, 'I can start over every day,'" said Kieran. "It took me years to figure that out. I repeated it to myself so many times that eventually I believed it."

"Mindfulness can help you notice and acknowledge your stressful thoughts—the first step toward coming to terms with them—so that they no longer overwhelm you." *RyanJLane/E+ via Getty Images*

Mindfulness

Mindfulness practice has become a hot topic lately, because people like Emma Watson and Anderson Cooper are into it, and there's been a lot of research that shows that it really works. Mindfulness practice generally includes meditation and other exercises, the goal of which is to increase awareness of one's thoughts, feelings, and experiences in the present moment—that is, to be *mindful* of what is going through your head and pay attention to it, without judging it. Do you keep thinking about that fight you had with your best friend, replaying every detail? Rather than trying to push away those thoughts or telling yourself not to think about the fight, a mindfulness approach would be to take a (mental) step back and just notice that you are thinking about this. Notice how your body feels—jaw clenched, shoulders hunched over. Notice your feelings—stress, anger, hurt, and so on. Notice where your mind went to next: "Will my other friends think the fight was my fault?"

According to psychologist Dr. Steven C. Hayes, the emotional distress we experience occurs because we become fused with our thoughts; we do not have that distance from them. For example, when we think "I am bad," we really feel that we *are* bad, not just that we're having that thought.[7] With this fog of stressful thoughts and feelings swirling around us, we are trapped. We can't see a clear path out of the fog, nor can we even focus on what's right in front of us—our lives! We are so caught up ruminating in this fog—with our minds going a million miles an hour—we are missing out on everything around us. The purpose of mindfulness is to help clear this fog by drawing our attention to it and giving us a little distance from all these thoughts and feelings. The idea is not to push the thoughts away (which doesn't work); it is just to notice them and acknowledge them, which is the first step toward coming to terms with them.

Mindfulness practice can be used in conjunction with most other kinds of therapies (cognitive behavioral therapy, psychodynamic therapy, etc.), practiced in a group, or just learned individually. If you are interested in learning some mindfulness tools on your own, there are lots of apps—such as Headspace—that can give you the background information and teach you the skills to get started with some mindfulness practices.

The downside? It sounds easier than it is. Mindfulness is hard. And if your brain is overloaded with anxiety and moving a million miles an hour, it's even harder. We know anxiety hampers our ability to sit still and pay attention and that's exactly what mindfulness is asking us to do. Dr. Andersen, who teaches mindfulness to high school students, has practiced mindfulness himself for decades, but acknowledges that it is a difficult thing to get into. He recommends that teens practice mindfulness in a group so that they have a community to support their practice (peer pressure in a good way?); this will make you more likely to stick with it.

Self-Help Books/Workbooks

Self-help books can be a good way to learn strategies for dealing with anxiety. The downside? These strategies may be really hard to implement without other people—like a therapist or community—to support you. But if you want to give it a try, here are some good resources:

- *The Anxiety Survival Guide for Teens* by Jennifer Shannon, LMFT
- *My Anxious Mind: A Teen's Guide to Managing Anxiety and Panic* by Michael A. Tompkins, PhD, and Katherine Martinez, PsyD
- *The Anxiety Workbook for Teens: Activities to Help You Deal with Anxiety and Worry* by Lisa M. Schab, LCSW

Other Tools: What Works for You?

- Deep breathing (or belly breathing)
- Progressive muscle relaxation
- Visualization
- Exercise
- Getting creative! Try art, singing, dancing, doodling, or cooking

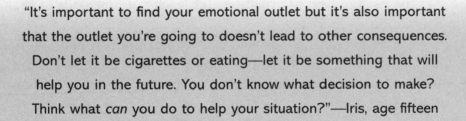

"It's important to find your emotional outlet but it's also important that the outlet you're going to doesn't lead to other consequences. Don't let it be cigarettes or eating—let it be something that will help you in the future. You don't know what decision to make? Think what *can* you do to help your situation?"—Iris, age fifteen

Humor

Humor is usually the last thing on your mind when you're anxious, but for many people, it can be a helpful strategy in giving anxiety the boot. There's a reason they say "laughter is the best medicine." With all those positive endorphins it releases into your brain, laughter forces you into a better frame of mind. It's generally pretty difficult to be anxious when you're laughing (and there's not a more relaxed feeling in the world then after you've laughed yourself to tears). For all you Harry Potter fans, think about the boggart that Harry had to face—that shape-shifting creature that turns into your worst nightmare. The only way to defeat a boggart is to cast a spell ("Riddikulus") that will transform the boggart from something scary into something funny. "If the caster is able to laugh aloud at the boggart, it will disappear at once," explains one website. "The intention is to force the boggart to assume a less-threatening and hopefully comical form."[8] For Neville Longbottom, the boggart takes the shape of his strictest professor, Severus Snape. The only way he can dispel the creature is to make the haunting vision funny: Severus Snape wearing a dress. J. K. Rowling is no psychologist, but her antidote to fearful things rings true for many people. Think about how you can make the subject of your anxiety more comical. (Of course, this requires you to first pinpoint what some of your worst nightmares are.) If your worst nightmare is a failing grade on a test, try to picture that F written in hearts or emojis. Or your teacher rapping "Baby Got Back" when she hands the test back to you. If you find yourself starting to smile at this idea, then using humor may be a great strategy for you. If you're reading this and wondering why on earth I'm talking about a teacher and Sir Mixalot, then move on to the next section.

Find Your Mantra

Whether it's a song lyric or something you heard, find a saying that speaks to you. Many teenagers I spoke with had found something that hit home for them. One girl, Iris, has a ring with the saying "Don't complain that the roses have thorns; be grateful that the thorn bushes have roses," which has helped her to keep up a positive attitude. A mantra that spoke to Hayley is "Thoughts are thoughts, and actions are what really count." She was reassured in remembering that the overwhelming and worrisome thoughts she was having did not define her. One of my personal favorites: "So far you've survived 100 percent of your worst days. You're doing great" (author unknown). Find what speaks to you.

Chelsea's Story, Part 2: The Treatment That Worked

Like many anxious people, Chelsea is a planner, so she generally feels calmer when she can regain some sense of control over the situation that is making her anxious. When working with a therapist briefly last year, Chelsea remembers the therapist giving her a worksheet in which she had to write down what was wrong, and the steps needed to fix it. First Chelsea wrote down the things that were bothering her and the main areas of stress. Then she brainstormed the end point—how did she want to come out from this stress? "I like having steps," said Chelsea. "It was very helpful."

Chelsea generally takes this approach to dealing with all aspects of her life—what steps can she take to reduce her anxiety? When she starts breathing heavily, she tries to control her breathing—breathing in for six seconds, breathing out for five seconds—until the feeling passes. In social situations, Chelsea tries to plan ahead by strategizing who she will talk to, and in what order (sometimes there are even graphs involved in the planning!). She even comes prepared with three to five conversation starters, in case the conversation dies down. "I don't like to be unprepared," Chelsea said.

Another strategy that she has found helpful is writing letters to her future self, filled with advice and perspective. "You hear the advice that other people give you, but no one knows you better than yourself," said Chelsea. "I remind my [future] self that this is all in my head."

Most of all, Chelsea has found that mindset is key. "When I had a really pessimistic, down mindset, I was having a bad time," she said, "but if I wake up and think, 'Today's going to be a good day,' it's going to be fine. So that's something I'm really going to hold on to."

Although she feels that she has successfully managed her anxiety up this point, Chelsea has decided to explore the option of seeing a therapist for the coming school year. Her goal is to be more confident in who she is, and feel some relief from the physical symptoms of anxiety she experiences.

"When you experience hard times, sometimes pushing through isn't always the answer. You know what your limits are. You know when you have to take a step back," said Chelsea. It is advice that she has given other people before, but she herself finds it hard to follow. "I've never been good at confronting people. I like to be a pleaser. . . . I want to feel depended on. But all that responsibility gets to you—it gets in your head and it's too much sometimes."

Conclusion

Unlike some of the other kinds of anxiety this book talks about, generalized anxiety is a hard problem to pinpoint for several reasons. First, many of the things you worry about may feel (and may be!) quite legitimate, making it hard to discern when the anxiety is warranted and when it is not. Second, you may not even have a reason for that general sense of worry you feel—somehow it is all just too much (even if you don't know what "it" is). But when you feel the anxiety impinging on your life, as Hayley, Kieran, and Chelsea did, it is time for a change. As you saw with these girls, the path to treating anxiety is extremely individualistic. You may love individual therapy, or you may hate it. You may find a self-help book that speaks to you, or you may find them aggravating and distinctly unhelpful. Perhaps none of these stories or strategies resonated with you and you feel like you will never get out from under the anxiety cloud. But you will—it may just take some time to find the right path.

PANIC DISORDER

Unlike generalized anxiety disorder, which may feel a bit nebulous, you would know with some certainty if you have experienced a panic attack. Many people use the term *panic* loosely, when they're talking about being stressed or worried about something. But in a true panic attack, you do not feel stressed or worried. You feel like you're either dying or completely losing your mind—that something is just horribly, horribly wrong, and no one will convince you otherwise. Psychologists Dr. David Clark and Dr. Aaron Beck call it a "tsunami of anxiety." Author Hal Mathew describes it as a train running over you. "In a matter of seconds," he writes, "you went from being a normal person having a normal day to becoming the most desperate creature on the planet."[1] By all accounts, it's bad. If anxiety is the body's alarm system sounding false alarms, then panic attacks are the body's alarm system gone completely haywire.

belterz/E+ via Getty Images

In this chapter, we will discuss the definition of panic attacks, some diagnoses that go along with them, symptoms and treatment, and accounts of some very brave people who have suffered from panic attacks and lived to tell the tale.

Definition and Symptoms

According to the fifth edition of the *Diagnostic and Statistical Manual of Mental Disorders (DSM-5)*, a panic attack is defined as "an abrupt surge of intense fear or intense discomfort that reaches a peak within minutes."[2] During a panic attack, you must experience at least four of the following physical or cognitive symptoms:

Physical symptoms (symptoms followed by an asterisk [★] are most likely to be reported by adolescents, according to one study):[3]

- Palpitations, pounding heart, or accelerated heart rate★
- Sweating
- Trembling or shaking★
- Sensations of shortness of breath or smothering
- Feelings of choking
- Chest pain or discomfort
- Nausea or abdominal distress★
- Feeling dizzy, unsteady, light-headed, or faint
- Chills or heat sensations★
- Paresthesias (numbness or tingling sensations)

Cognitive symptoms:

- Derealization (feelings of unreality) or depersonalization (being detached from oneself)
- Fear of losing control or "going crazy"
- Fear of dying

We've all seen panic attacks portrayed in movies and TV shows. In *Sex and the City*, we see Carrie Bradshaw (played by Sarah Jessica Parker) experience a panic attack when trying on a frumpy wedding dress. "Oh my god, this is too tight, I can't breathe," she gasps. And then, panting and collapsing to the floor: "I'm not kidding, get it off, I'm burning up, I can't breathe."[4] More recently, Rhonda Rittenhouse had a panic attack in *The Bachelor* (for which they called the paramedics), Randall Pearson (played by Sterling K. Brown) has panic attacks in *This Is Us*, Richard Hendricks (played by Thomas Middleditch) has panic attacks in *Silicon Valley*, and even the great Tony Stark (played by Robert Downey Jr.) has panic attacks in *Iron Man 3*. Hey, even superheroes are susceptible.

Diagnoses

There are two diagnoses that include panic attacks—panic disorder and agoraphobia—and we'll discuss each one.

"This black hole is what my panic feels like. It's like a downward spiral of 'Ahhhh!'" *Artist: Rebecka Grunberg*

Panic Disorder

If you have a diagnosis of panic disorder, it means that you have "recurrent, un-expected panic attacks"[5] which cannot be attributed to other medical conditions or side effects of substances. (In other words, if you only panic when you smoke pot, that's something different.) In addition, following a panic attack, you need to have experienced one or both of the following:

- Persistent worry about having more panic attacks *or* worry about the conse-quences of panic attacks (e.g., you are scared you will have a heart attack)
- "A significant maladaptive change in behavior related to the attacks"[6]

Translation of this diagnosis: you keep having panic attacks, you worry con-stantly about having panic attacks, and as a result, you've started to avoid things that may bring on a panic attack. For example, your heart started racing and you couldn't breathe. Terrible, scary feeling. Ever since that, you find yourself avoid-ing activities that would lead to shortness of breath—goodbye Zumba class!

Psychologist Dr. Julian Herskowitz, who runs an anxiety treatment center in Long Island, told me that panic disorder is the most common problem that brings teenagers in for treatment. "The most common age of onset is sixteen to eighteen. It can lead to school phobia, restrictions, secondary depression," he explained. His colleague, psychologist Dr. Cassandra D'Accordo, added, "And that gets parents' attention. It's so distressing that you can't ignore it anymore."

When people describe their panic attacks to me, the most common themes are that they feel like they are going crazy or losing control, or they feel like they are going to die. One woman I spoke with was ready to call an ambulance when she found herself collapsed on the floor, breathing heavily, and feeling like her chest was closing. "I sincerely genuinely thought that was the end of my life," she said. Another woman went to the emergency room when she started experiencing numb-ness on one side of her body. "I was convinced I had a blood clot," she explained.

! Nocturnal Panic Attacks

Nocturnal panic attacks refer to when you wake up in a state of panic, which can be equally frightening. "I've had it happen a few times over the years," one woman told me. "It's so scary. It happens when I sleep. . . . I wake up already in a panic. I feel like I can't breathe. I feel like I'm dying. I wake up and [my] heart's pounding. I rush to the bathroom and drink water in a panicked state. It's really crazy."

What Causes Panic Disorder?

- *Age.* Although some children and teenagers experience panic attacks, the rates of panic disorder increase throughout adolescence and peak when you reach early adulthood. That means that you are more likely to be diagnosed with panic disorder in your late teens or early twenties. If you're still a younger teenager right now, stay tuned . . .

- *Environmental factors.* Even if it may seem like a panic attack came out of nowhere, research shows that they are often associated with stressful life events—for example, something stressful having to do with family, friends, illness, or academics, just to name a few.[a] Stressful or traumatic events from earlier in childhood (like abuse or even separation anxiety) can also be a risk factor. So even if you think your panic attack has nothing at all to do with your recent breakup or your parents fighting, chances are that there's some connection there worth thinking about.

- *Genetics.* Same ol' story. Studies have shown that a family history of panic disorder or panic attacks is a common predictor. The same is true if a parent has anxiety, depression, or bipolar disorder. If one or both of your parents has one of these conditions, those pesky genes might be to blame for your panic attacks.

- *Temperament.* According to the *DSM-5*, a bunch of personality traits like negative affectivity (how prone you are to experiencing negative emotions) and anxiety sensitivity (how prone you are to being freaked out by anxiety symptoms) may be risk factors for developing panic disorder. Basically, we're all wired differently. Some people are prone to getting angry or depressed; you might just be more prone to getting anxious. And of course, if you've always had a history of panicky-like symptoms as a kid, that doesn't bode well either.

"Later I told my therapist, and she asked me why I didn't call her. I said, 'Because why would I call a psychiatrist for what I thought was a blood clot!'"

Agoraphobia

After you've experienced a bad panic attack, your gut reaction might be to avoid any situation which may cause that to happen again. If it happened at the grocery store, kiss that Shop Rite goodbye! If it happened at a party, you may start to feel like staying home on the weekends is your best bet in life. "All you know for certain," writes Hal Mathew—a journalist and social worker who suffered from panic disorder and agoraphobia himself—"is that you never, ever want to have one of those [panic attacks] again. From now on, each time you venture out, you have to be constantly alert to this gruesome new threat. You begin to avoid places or circumstances that might cause another panic attack, but the attacks persist. You continue to eliminate possible triggers and finally there are places you can no longer go and things you can no longer do."[7]

To be diagnosed with agoraphobia, you need to be extremely anxious about and attempt to avoid at least two of the following situations:

- Using public transportation
- Being in wide open spaces, like a parking lot
- Being in enclosed places, like a store or movie theater
- Standing in line, or being in a crowd
- Being outside of your home by yourself[8]

Why are you attempting to avoid these situations? Because the thought that you might be in one of these places, start panicking, and then have no way out is literally your worst nightmare. Just the thought of going shopping at the mall makes your heart pound. And that's not even on Black Friday!

Because panic attacks are so intense and debilitating, panic disorder and agoraphobia can cause a lot more of a disturbance in your life than, say, a fear

What Causes Agoraphobia?

The causes of agoraphobia are pretty much the same as panic disorder—your age, personality traits, stressful things going on in your life, and all that jazz. Notably, agoraphobia also has a very strong link to genetics as a risk factor. So, if one of your parents has agoraphobia, you have a really high chance of inheriting it.

Karen's Story

Although Karen had struggled with anxiety throughout her adolescence, she did not have her first panic attack until the year that she graduated college, at age twenty-two. "I remember when I first started having full blown panic attacks, I was thinking, 'Where did this come from?!'" recalled Karen. "And then you realize when you start going to therapy that this has actually been happening for a very long time, just not that bad." In high school, Karen remembers crying hysterically until she couldn't breathe if she was late to class or hadn't finished an assignment, but she had never received a formal diagnosis or sought out any treatment for her anxiety.

Then, at the start of a graduate program abroad, Karen started to feel a tingling sensation in her hand that would not go away. Karen became increasingly alarmed as the tingling then spread to her foot and she started having bad headaches. "That's when I totally freaked out and was like 'Oh my god, I'm having a stroke! Is it a stroke or a heart attack?" Karen said. "I called the emergency number, and they took me to the emergency room and couldn't find anything. I just remember being there and saying, 'You're telling me nothing is wrong, but I'm telling you something is terribly wrong.'"

No less agitated, Karen returned home from the hospital, where she continued to experience the same symptoms: tingling and headaches. Increasingly, she had trouble concentrating and was afraid to be alone, in case she needed someone to call an ambulance. This continued for months, with Karen actually calling an ambulance on several occasions.

Determined to get to the bottom of it, Karen underwent test after test—CT scans, MRIs, EKGs, and blood tests—all of which came back with normal results. She tried getting massages, doing guided meditation, getting acupuncture, and consulting with an infectious disease specialist, but nothing was helping. Finally, a neurologist she was seeing suggested that Karen might have depression. The diagnosis did not seem right. "But I'm not depressed!" thought Karen. "It didn't make any sense to me."

For some people with agoraphobia, the thought that they might be in a crowded place, start panicking, and then have no way out is literally their worst nightmare. *Tero Vesalainen/ istock via Getty Images*

of flying. To avoid panic attacks, you may end up frequently missing school, as well as other fun things like extracurricular activities or social events. For many teens, fears of various places and things can make their worlds smaller and smaller, until staying in their house is just about the only place that feels safe (and sometimes not even that). And staying at home all day may help you feel in control for the moment, but it will also significantly cramp your lifestyle. If this sort of thing sounds familiar and has been going for six months or more, chances are you have agoraphobia.

It is important to note that it is very rare for people to only experience panic disorder or agoraphobia, with no other concerns. More often than not, if you're experiencing panic attacks, you've probably got some other stuff going on, like depression or another anxiety disorder. For more on that, see chapter 8.

Treatment

If you are suffering from panic attacks, you probably want to just make them stop as soon as humanly possible. There are several things that can help with managing panic attacks—therapy, medication, and so on, which we will discuss next—but many professionals say that the key to stopping panic is actually changing the way you think about it. You cannot prevent a panic attack from starting, but you can alter its course by how you handle it. Dr. Martin Seif, a psychologist who has treated anxiety for over thirty-five years, explained it to me as follows. "I'm going to ask you to push my hand," he said, and then held up his own hand against mine. "Push as hard as you can!" Then Dr. Seif pulled his hand away and my hand fell forward.

"Why did you stop?" he asked.

"Because you stopped!" I replied.

"Exactly," he said. "That's the way I want you to think about anxiety. You keep pushing back against anxiety and it'll push against you. You need to stop pushing."

But how do you "stop pushing" when you're overwhelmed with panic? Psychologists Dr. Michael A. Tompkins and Dr. Katherine Martinez use the metaphor of a rip current. Rip currents are strong tides that pull you away from the shore and set you adrift at sea. But if you struggle to swim against a rip current back toward the shore, you will ultimately just exhaust yourself and subsequently drown. So, the strategy that lifeguards recommend is to just relax and stay afloat when you are caught in a rip current. "A rip current does not pull you under . . . so you are safe so long as you float," Tompkins and Martinez explain. "Soon the current will die out and you are free to swim into shore."[9] So too with panic attacks. The more you struggle against them, the more they will wear you down and overtake you. Instead, if you can learn to ride the "panic wave" and stay afloat until it passes, then it cannot harm you. "It is very important to understand," explain Tompkins and Martinez, "that trying to fight the initial feelings of panic is 90% of the problem."[10]

"The concept is, do the opposite of what anxiety tells you," Dr. Seif told me. "When anxiety tells you 'Hold on! Grab the seat!' you've got to let go."

Hal Mathews echoes this sentiment as well: "Your job is to completely and totally reverse everything about fear that controls you now. . . . It means totally letting down your guard and allowing the thing you dread the most to come sit beside you on the couch."[11] (For inspiration on the idea of doing the opposite with a little comic relief, watch the episode of *Seinfeld* titled "The Opposite.") By taking this counterintuitive approach, you can start to lessen the overwhelming feeling of being consumed by panic and start to be able to ride it out instead.

For many people, a key step is learning about panic disorder and gaining the understanding that panic attacks aren't actually dangerous (even though they feel dangerous). This is also something that is counterintuitive. Experience has taught us that things like hyperventilating, dizziness, or a racing heart mean that something is *wrong* with you. So, the fact that these things can happen without anything actually being wrong is bizarre. When people go to the emergency room because of a panic attack, they are often shocked and disbelieving to hear that there is nothing physically wrong, and they often seek out multiple medical opinions. However, in the case of panic disorder, it's true! There isn't anything physically wrong; it is just another example of your mind interpreting something in a way that is frightening (see chapter 1 for more about how our brains are so darn good at freaking us out). Just having that fact stored in the back of your mind can be helpful, when panic rears its ugly head. Even though it feels like something is wrong, your body is safe and you are safe. "This is panic," you can remind yourself, as you ride that wave. "It cannot harm me, physically or mentally." No one has ever died or gone crazy from having a panic attack. As psychologist Dr. Tamar E. Chansky puts it, "The more you understand how panic works, the more you will be able to label what is going on. . . . This takes the attack out of the crisis category and turns it into a manageable situation whose resolution is not a matter of life or death but just a matter of time."[12]

Exposure Therapy

The basic premise of exposure therapy (also called systematic desensitization) is that you gradually—or sometimes not so gradually—expose yourself to the thing that freaks you out. See chapter 5 for a more detailed explanation of how exactly that works. In the case of specific phobias (chapter 5), the thing that freaks you out may be dogs or needles or flying in an airplane. In the case of panic disorder and agoraphobia, it is a little different; the thing that freaks you out might be a situation that triggers panic (e.g., waiting in line, going to a crowded area, etc.), or it might be the actual symptoms of panic (feeling breathless, dizzy, and so on). Once you have figured out the triggers, the process is the same: a therapist will help gradually expose you to them in a manageable way. With the support of the therapist and the strategies he or she teaches you, you will find that you are slowly able to build up a tolerance for the things you had been doggedly avoiding. It may take a while before you're back in Zumba, but after enough brisk walks back and forth to the mailbox, Zumba may seem a lot more doable than it did before. Becoming short of breath (or whatever your trigger is) will no longer fill you with dread that you're dying.

Medication

For panic disorder or agoraphobia, there are two possible routes that involve medication. The first is taking a medication every day that reduces your overall susceptibility to anxiety and panic. These medications are the same ones we mentioned in chapter 3: SSRIs (selective serotonin reuptake inhibitors) and SNRIs (serotonin-norepinephrine reuptake inhibitors) such as Prozac, Paxil, Zoloft, Lexapro, Celexa, Cymbalta, Effexor, and so on. (For more on how those work, see chapter 7.) These medications can lower your anxiety overall but won't help you if you're in a full-blown panic.

"But then there are the panic attacks. If it weren't for the moments of panic, the tears, the hyperventilation, I wouldn't consider taking medication. I've done better than average. I'm not just 'getting by.' But even one of those is far too many."—Laura, age twenty-two

That brings us to the second medication route, which includes anti-anxiety medications known as benzodiazepines. The most common benzodiazepines prescribed to teenagers are Xanax, Klonopin, Valium, and Ativan. Benzodiazepines are good at reducing panic and anxiety symptoms in the moment. Many teenagers like to have this type of medication with them as a safety precaution—especially if they know they'll be in a situation that may elicit panic symptoms. "It's easier to go on a tightrope if you know there's a net," psychologist Dr. Julian Herskowitz told me. "But I tell [patients] to take it only if all else fails."

Benzodiazepines might sound like the silver bullet you've been looking for, so what is the downside? Since benzodiazepines can work like a charm in the moment, it's easy to become dependent on them, and that's not good. First, they are highly addictive. Second, relying on them to take away the panic won't allow you to learn and practice the strategies you need to understand the root causes of the panic and get the proper treatment. It's fine to take Tylenol to get rid of a headache, but if your headache continues day after day, you'd want to do more than just keep taking Tylenol. You'd want to get that problem checked out and properly treated! So too with anxiety and panic. As psychiatrist Dr. Elizabeth Ortiz-Schwartz explained it to me, "The goal of medication treatment is to decrease the anxiety 'til it becomes more manageable, not to take it away altogether. You want to try to get it to a sweet spot where [you] feel motivated and wanting to do better, but not paralyzed by high levels of anxiety."

Self-Help Books/Workbooks

Self-help books can be a good way to learn strategies for dealing with panic. Most people report that when you are actually experiencing a panic attack, self-help books won't help you at all. But once you are back to your rational self, many books offer good tips and advice about how to get rid of panic symptoms and all the issues (like agoraphobia) that come with them. Here is a good resource to start with:

- *The Panic Workbook for Teens: Breaking the Cycle of Fear, Worry and Panic Attacks* by Debra Kissen, PhD, MHSA; Bari Goldman Cohen, PhD; and Kathi Fine Abitbol, PhD

Rule Out Medical Concerns

Since many symptoms of panic are physical ones (heavy breathing, feeling dizzy, chills, and so on), it is important to establish that there's not a different medical reason why you're experiencing these symptoms. Psychologist Dr. Dan Villiers, a founder of the Anxiety Institute in Connecticut, told me that approximately two out of every ten students he evaluates for treatment present with very typical anxiety symptoms that are actually caused by a medical or physiological condition. He noted that sometimes a medical condition is the sole cause of the symptoms (e.g., thyroid conditions, allergic reactions, and so on) and sometimes a medical condition may be co-occurring with anxiety (e.g., asthma, migraines, or irritable bowel syndrome, among others). For example, Dr. Villiers recently had a college student seek treatment for panic attacks; however, the assessment and subsequent referral to a neurologist revealed that the student actually had a traumatic brain injury. So best to check in with your doctor before you jump into any kind of treatment, so she can confirm that it's anxiety you're experiencing and not something else. See chapter 7 for more on this.

Other Strategies

Although therapy and medication are considered the mainstays of treatment for panic disorder, there are many other strategies that you may find helpful in your day-to-day life. Try them and see what works for you.

- *Make contact.* Find people! Sometimes just sitting in the same room as someone else or going for a walk with someone can quell oncoming feelings of panic. Find the people you feel most comfortable with and use them as a resource.[13]
- *Exercise.* This is a tricky one, since things like heavy breathing, heart racing, and so on are often what trigger panic attacks in the first place. So don't just crank up a treadmill to the highest setting if you're not ready for that. However, exercise is good for endorphins, which is good for getting

rid of anxiety, so try doing some relaxation and strengthening exercises to start with, and then work your way up from there.

- *Find something funny.* Fighting back against panic is a serious job, making you tense from the minute you wake up until the minute you fall asleep. Try to break this cycle by watching funny videos or doing anything that makes you laugh. Research has shown that laughing is another good way to boost endorphins (the feel-good brain chemicals), which helps to relieve pain and stress (see the part in chapter 3 about humor). YouTube has made this ridiculously easy; no shortage of funny stuff on there. Keep watching until you've had some really good belly laughs.[14]

- *Focus on your environment.* This is called a "grounding technique" in therapy. When we get too much in our heads, it can be helpful to force your brain to focus on the mundane details of the world around you. Notice what the floor feels like under your feet, the texture of the couch you're sitting on, the different colors on the walls around you, and so on. If your brain is starting to go haywire, this can be a good way to stay grounded in the present and not let the feelings of panic spiral out of control.

- *Smell something.* Similarly to the last bullet point, the practice of aromatherapy (smelling essential oils) can have a calming effect for many people. For panic, the aromatherapy community recommends lavender or sandalwood, and some people find lemon-scented things helpful as well. Many people have told me that just trying to focus on what they're smelling (whether it's scented or not) can refocus their minds and detract from the panic.

- *Deep breathing.* Slow down your breathing. Count to four while you breathe in and to five while you breathe out. Make sure you are breathing in all the way down to your diaphragm. Watch your belly go up and down while you breathe. For some people breathing techniques work like a charm in calming down their bodies. There are many apps that can help with this. One example is Breathe2Relax, which gives you a nice visual aid to focus on while you are taking deep breaths in and out.

- *Cold water.* Because human beings are mammals, we have something called the "mammalian diving reflex." The basic idea is that when cold water hits our face, our bodies automatically prepare for an underwater dive—we do things like slow down our heart rate and conserve oxygen (this reflex happens in ducks and seals too before they dive under the water). What does this have to do with panic? If your body is starting to panic and your sympathetic nervous system is kicking in, you may be able to nip it in the bud by dunking your face in cold water a couple of times. Most people immediately feel the results as their heart rate starts to decrease and their breathing slows down.

- *Look for patterns.* For people who have had multiple panic attacks, or panic attacks with some frequency, they may be able to identify certain signs that a panic attack is starting. It may be because you're in a situation that you know triggers panic (for example, a crowded room or somewhere more specific like the dentist's office). Or it may be a feeling you get as you sense your body starting to rev up—similar to the way people feel a migraine coming on. If you can identify that feeling early on, you may be able to temper the course or duration of the panic attack and start using some coping skills right off the bat.

Karen's Story, Part 2: The Treatment That Worked

Although Karen's symptoms had somewhat subsided by the time she returned to the United States several months later, she still felt uncomfortable with the diagnosis of depression. "But what was I going to do?" explained Karen. "It didn't make sense to keep going back to the ER." Karen continued therapy with a new therapist and was given a prescription for Klonopin, although she was too anxious to take it. "That summer, there were nights that I couldn't fall asleep and I was just shaking," Karen recalled. "I couldn't fall asleep because I couldn't shut down. I understood enough to know that nothing was really wrong. I just *felt* like things were wrong."

It wasn't until three years later, when Karen began seeing a new therapist, that things began to make sense to her. "I just happened to get the right sort of therapist who actually read through the *DSM* descriptions, and I was like 'Oh! Panic disorder! That's what actually lines up with my symptoms!'" Finally, Karen felt she had a clear diagnosis that matched her experiences. "This makes sense in a way that the diagnosis of depression didn't. It felt wrong and so I didn't quite trust what [previous] therapists were staying in terms of what to do. Once it started to make sense it became easier to deal with."

While Karen continued therapy, she also sought out psychiatric help and soon began taking Prozac to treat her anxiety. "Within a couple days it felt like a weight had been lifted off my chest. I literally could breathe again. I've not had a panic attack since then." Just as Dr. Seif described it, Karen no longer felt like she had to push back against the anxiety and that understanding gave her newfound calm.

Conclusion

Author Hal Mathews wrote of panic, "This is one of life's crueler realizations: you suddenly discover that your body came equipped with a kick-ass state-of-the-art alarm system, but you can't find any instructions on how to turn the screeching thing off."[15] Panic is a tricky beast to deal with for several reasons. First, it can be completely terrifying and debilitating. Second, unlike a phobia, it can be hard to know what triggers it since most people have the feeling that their panic attack came out of nowhere. Third, and perhaps most confusing, it often does not even feel like anxiety (it feels like something much worse!), which makes it hard to identify in the first place and get the proper treatment. So, if you have already discovered that panic disorder or agoraphobia is what you have, then you've taken a giant step in the right direction. Seeing panic for what it is—and not some terrifying, life-ending health crisis—will go a long way toward being able to cope with it effectively. Your next step will be finding the right combination of strategies to employ—whether that includes therapy, medication, aromatherapy oils, or any number of things. Don't feel bad about asking for help—from your parents, a school counselor, a therapist—and don't feel bad if you can't cure your panic attacks overnight. It may take some soul searching in therapy and some trial and error with other strategies, but there will be relief in your future!

SPECIFIC PHOBIAS

Not to state the obvious, but specific phobias are, well, incredibly specific: butterflies, elevators, having blood drawn, being in a small space, and so on. It's not like generalized anxiety (see chapter 3) where people may feel a lingering sense of unease and not be sure why. In this case, you would definitely know why you are anxious.

Definition and Symptoms

According to the fifth edition of the *Diagnostic and Statistical Manual of Mental Disorders (DSM-5)*, the phobic object or situation causes immediate fear or anxiety in the person, which is out of proportion to the actual threat caused by the object or situation. That means that if you're jogging in the Sahara, come face-to-face with a lion and completely freak out, you do *not* have a phobia of lions. You *should* be freaking out! But if you always freak out just by seeing a picture of a lion and this has been going on for more than six months, you probably have a specific phobia. The other criterion you need for getting a diagnosis is that the fear, anxiety, or avoidance of the thing needs to be causing serious problems in your life—making you freak out, getting in the way of social plans, or other things that totally disrupt your life. You might say "I have a phobia of butterflies!" but if it doesn't really affect your life and you can get along just fine without butterflies, then I wouldn't worry about it. But if you're now refusing to go outside from April until October, just in case a butterfly flies by, you should keep reading this chapter.

The *DSM-5* lists several categories of specific phobias:

- Animal (spiders, insects, dogs, etc.)
- Natural environment (storms, heights, water)
- Blood-injury-injection (needles, invasive medical procedures)
- Situational (airplanes, elevators, enclosed places)
- Other (e.g., situations that may lead to choking or vomiting; for children, loud sounds or costumed characters; etc.)

Artist: Chana Rosa Bogart

Fear of flying is a common specific phobia. *martin-dm/E+ via Getty Images*

You may only have one of the phobias on this list. However, it is more common to have more than one specific phobia. In fact, most people with a specific phobia have at least three. I've had teenagers come to my office saying they have a fear of flying, but then it turns out they're also freaked out by dogs and thunderstorms.

What Causes Specific Phobias?

We don't know exactly what causes specific phobias. Two people could have the exact same experience (flying on a plane with lots of turbulence) and one is fine and the other develops a lifelong fear of flying. It's hard to predict, but here are some factors that may contribute:

- *Genetics.* Specific phobias aren't exactly inherited directly (there's no gene or chromosome for fear of flying), but since certain personality traits that contribute to anxiety are heritable (see chapter 3), if your parents are pretty anxious or have phobias, that might be a contributing factor.

- *Negative experiences and learning.* Almost a century ago, psychologists like Ivan Pavlov and John Watson researched how animals and humans learned to be excited about or afraid of new things. In one experiment, Watson showed a baby—whose nickname was "Little Albert"—a small animal like a rat or rabbit, and Little Albert was perfectly happy. But when Watson rang a loud bell while showing him the rat, Little Albert freaked out and started to cry. With enough startling bell ringing, Little Albert learned that being around one of those furry animals was bad news, and he started to fear rats, even without the sound of a bell. That is, he became afraid of something that wasn't initially scary just because of an experience that was a little scary. Hello, phobia! The same thing can happen to us. Maybe we were on a plane (not scary) and felt some turbulence (scary) or saw a plane crash in a movie (scary), and suddenly we are scared of planes. Think back if you've ever had any negative experiences with the thing that you're afraid of.[a]

- *Observation.* Have you ever seen someone totally freak out about something, and then suddenly you're not feeling so confident about it either? Sometimes we develop phobias just by watching someone else, even if we never had a bad experience ourselves. I had an adult friend who would always yell at her kids, "*Stay away from dogs! They might bite you!*" anytime a dog was nearby. It's not a mystery where her son's phobia of dogs came from.

- *"Once = Always" rule.*[b] Whether it was originally something you observed or learned through experience, phobias tend to develop when we assume that one bad situation is the rule and not the exception. For example, one time a dog was snarling and aggressive and now you are convinced *all* dogs are that way. Or one time you got sick and threw up, and now you worry about it being a frequent possibility. When we take a mental step back, most people can acknowledge that once does *not* equal always—this is just probability overestimation. (See chapter 1 for more about this.) But like any cognitive distortion, it can be hard to see it that way initially. Our brains can be pretty convincing.

Julie's Story

Julie remembers being "a worrier" her whole life ("As a kid I wore three watches 'cause I was worried one would break!" Julie recalled), but it wasn't until she moved to New York City as a young adult that she developed a specific phobia: bedbugs.

If you have no idea what bedbugs are, they are tiny bloodsucking bugs that enjoy making their homes in human beds, couches, and other soft furniture. (If you're starting to develop your own phobia reading this, you can skip ahead to the next section.) While no New Yorker would welcome bedbugs, most shrug it off as one of the possible but unlikely hazards of living in a big city (along with things like having your purse stolen or getting stuck in an elevator). Sure, it makes you cringe to think about it, so most people don't really think about it.

For Julie, her phobia started when she got some bug bites on her feet and thought they looked different than regular mosquito bites. "I got it in my head that I'd been bitten all over my feet by a bedbug," recalled Julie, and she became completely preoccupied with the idea. Julie hired a company to check her apartment, and although they did not find bedbugs there, she was unconvinced. "I still threw out my futon," said Julie. "But even after that, I couldn't let it go. I became consumed by the idea that I had bedbugs in my apartment." Julie began habitually checking for bedbugs under her bed every night, and she became afraid to sleep in hotels for fear that there would be bedbugs there as well. Whenever she found a bug of any kind in her apartment, she was convinced it was a bedbug. "I went to school and thought they were there. I went to my sister's house in Florida and thought I'd brought them with me. It just fed into itself more and more and just became an obsession," remembered Julie. "I was convinced that I was right! That I really had bedbugs! I had a 'bug place' and any time I found any bug in my apartment ever, I would bring my bug to them. And my sister would say 'Julie, you're obsessing.' And I'd say, 'I need them to check for me!' For a good year, I was probably in denial."

"I couldn't let it go. I became consumed by the idea that I had bedbugs in my apartment."
Lokibaho/istock via Getty Images

"Let the rain come down, whatever
You know storms don't last forever."
—song lyrics by Niels Geusebroek

Treatment

The good news about specific phobias is that they're usually very treatable. Unlike that pesky generalized anxiety, which can be a lifelong struggle, many people are able to get rid of specific phobias once and for all. In fact, many professionals I spoke with were inspired to do this kind of work because they themselves had been able to overcome fears and phobias that used to be debilitating. Psychologists Dr. Martin Seif and Dr. Julian Herskowitz had a phobia of flying and were both unable to fly for many years. Now they fly all over the world. For psychologist Dr. Dan Villiers, social anxiety and related fears of evaluation, judgment, and making mistakes stopped him from leaving his house for eight months (see chapter 6). Now he gives interviews on national television. It is pretty exciting to see how much treatment can help.

Many professionals recommend *exposure therapy* (also called "systematic desensitization") to treat specific phobias. Exposure therapy is based on the idea that it's impossible to remain uncomfortable with something if you're repeatedly exposed to it.[1] See the song lyric quoted earlier: storms don't last forever! And likewise, you can't freak out forever. Eventually, you will have to adapt, or habituate. For example, think about diving into a swimming pool. When you first dive in, the water feels cold. If you're like me, you spend the next ten minutes hopping and paddling around uncomfortably while your teeth chatter. But at a certain point, it's not cold anymore and it starts to feel quite comfortable (usually to the point that you don't want to get out of the pool!). This is the same phenomenon. Our bodies habituate. Just as you don't stay cold in a pool, you can't stay panicked in any given situation. Your body simply can't freak out indefinitely; eventually, it will adapt.

If this sounds terrifying, think about the fact that you've really been doing exposure therapy and habituating your whole life. When you were a little kid, you were probably scared of all kinds of things—turning off the lights, meeting your teacher on the first day of school, trying a new activity—which now wouldn't even cross your mind. Why? Because you got used to it. You habituated. The parts of your brain that were sounding the alarm eventually realized that no alarm was needed and started to settle down. The adrenaline that your body released in a moment of anxiety couldn't stay in your bloodstream indefinitely; after some period of time, it got reabsorbed back into cells or metabolized by enzymes in your blood.[2]

Dr. Steven Brodsky, a psychologist in New York City, will often ask patients, "Did you cross the street to come here today? Did you think very much about getting hit by a car?" Usually the answers are yes and no, respectively. But theoretically, crossing the street *is* something scary; certainly, children are often scared of it, and car accidents actually do lead to many premature deaths. Yet most of us are able to happily cross the street without a second thought. Why is that? "It's not because anyone convinced you it was safe to cross the street," Dr. Brodsky told me. "It's just the mere fact that you kept doing it! You started to become oblivious to it." In other words, after years and years of crossing the street, you simply habituated.

For specific phobias, exposure therapy will involve you doing the very things that freak you out: flying in an airplane, petting a dog, holding a spider, and so on. The way most treatments work is to gradually expose you to different aspects of the thing that frightens you, beginning with something that's not so scary and working your way up to facing your biggest fear. For example, if you are afraid of spiders, you would start by looking at pictures of spiders in a book. If even that was too much, you might start by looking at pictures of cartoon spiders or even just writing the word *spider*. Some therapists may start by making a chart known as an Exposure Hierarchy or Hierarchy of Fears (see p. 79). This list can include any number of situations, objects, thoughts, and so on, which will range from not scary at all, to the scariest thing you can imagine. Whereas items 1 and 2 on your Exposure Hierarchy may only make you cringe, the higher numbered items on the list will likely make you break into a cold sweat just thinking about them. Other therapists may not make the list initially but may just wing it and come up with new goals as you master old ones. Either way, the end goal is always the same: to work your way up to the point that you can do the thing you're afraid of and see that the world will not end. "We make our exposure therapy as gradual as it needs to be," Dr. Villiers explained to me. "The order depends on what the client feels ready for . . . each stage is a method to induce a 'just tolerable level' of anxiety until you are desensitized."

If you were following the hierarchy on p. 79, you would start by writing down the word *spiders*. Was it nerve-wracking but doable? If yes, you would do it again. (If this was not doable for you, your therapist would help you revisit your Exposure Hierarchy to add some less anxiety-inducing items). Then you would do it again. And again. You would continue doing it until all the anxiety is gone and frankly, you're starting to get a little bored. This means you have mastered the first step and are ready for the second. When you have mastered the second in the same way, you'd move on to the third, and so on. The key to exposure is repetition. Touching a spider once and then running out of the office to calm down in the hallway is not going to help anything. That won't convince your brain that the spider isn't dangerous; on the contrary, it will confirm in your mind that the

Sample Hierarchy of Fears: Fear of Spiders

1. Write down the word spider.
2. Look at pictures of cartoon spiders.
3. Look at pictures of spiders.
4. Watch movies of spiders.
5. See a live spider in a glass box from across the room.
6. Touch the box that the spider is in.
7. See a spider crawl around the room, outside of the box.
8. Stand next to the spider as it crawls around.
9. Touch the spider.
10. Hold the spider in your hand.

spider *is* dangerous, and you were lucky to survive such an encounter (and it's good you're a fast runner). Exposures need to be done over and over again until touching that spider feels as mundane as crossing the street (i.e., you barely notice it, and your mind wanders to what you're going to eat for dinner).

If your fear or phobia involves a body sensation (such as some of the things that we discussed in chapter 4, like heart pounding or shortness of breath), then your exposure would be to those very sensations. For example, you might run up a flight of stairs to expose yourself to the feeling of your heart rate going up. You might go on a carnival ride that makes you feel dizzy or slightly nauseous to expose yourself to that feeling. (If the mere suggestion of that makes you feel nauseous, then this is probably something that would be toward the top of your hierarchy.)

Sometimes a therapist will use the tactic of *imaginal exposure*. This is where you imagine the feared situation, without necessarily experiencing it in real life. This can work well for fears that are hard to reenact (for example, a fear of choking or throwing up in public). With this technique, the therapist might have you write down and read aloud your worst-case feared scenario, with every possible detail that makes you shiver to think about. After you have that written down or recorded, the therapist will have you read it or listen to it over and over again. At first, it may make your hair stand on end, but eventually, it won't have any effect on you. Hearing it repeatedly, you will become habituated and desensitized to even the scariest parts, stripping the fears of their power over you.

One thing to note is that mastering a fear does not mean that you're going to do a complete 180 and end up loving that thing. Will you be adopting a pet spider at the end of treatment? Signing up to get your pilot's license? Probably not. We're going for indifference here, not a newfound obsession. For example, having blood drawn used to send me into a complete panic (hysterical crying and screaming, you name it!). Now, after repeated exposure, I'm able to have blood drawn in a calm and composed fashion. I can't say that having blood drawn is one of my preferred activities, but the key thing is I am able to do it, without it sending me into a spiral of panic. And do I promise myself a large Starbucks drink to reward myself afterward? Yes, yes I do.

Checking Your Thoughts: The Cognitive Part of Treatment

Often used in conjunction with or in place of exposure therapy is something called cognitive restructuring—a method from cognitive behavioral therapy (see chapter 7)—to address some of the weird thoughts you may have about these fearful situations. For example, if you have a fear of dogs, you may have some pretty firm beliefs such as "All dogs are vicious," "Dogs will bite if they get the chance," "A dog could seriously injure me," "If a dog bites me, I'll die," and so on. If you don't have a fear of dogs, this probably sounds ridiculous to you, which

As with all anxiety, a key feature of specific phobias is that our instincts tell us to get the heck away from whatever is causing us to freak out, and then continue to avoid it at all costs. *bankrx/istock via Getty Images*

is how we know it's a distorted way of thinking. But if you *do* have a fear of dogs, these thoughts seem extremely accurate and worth paying attention to. In addition to doing actual exposure (hello, dog pictures), your therapist may work on helping you reevaluate some of these thoughts for accuracy and replace them with more realistic ideas.

To that end, many therapists recommend becoming an expert on the thing that frightens you. In chapter 7, you will learn about John, who had a fear of mummies. To alleviate this fear, John learned more about ancient Egypt. Not only does this help in the desensitization process (by page 20 of mummy pictures, they just don't hold the same effect), it can also help with the goal of getting your thinking to be more realistic. Having facts at your fingertips can help to dispel some of those nagging but misguided fears.

Avoidance and Safety Behaviors

As with all anxiety, a key feature of specific phobias is that our instincts tell us to get the heck away from whatever is causing us to freak out, and then continue to avoid it at all costs (see chapter 1). I've met people who spent their whole lives in their hometowns because they were too afraid to fly. This avoidance does not make any logical sense. Statistically, you're much more likely to die in a car accident than a plane crash, yet many people are happy to drive around all day, but break into a cold sweat when they see the airport.

The upside to avoidance is that it feels much better than anxiety. Good thing you're not in that uncomfortable situation anymore—phew! What a relief! "Avoidance is a very normal response," psychologist Dr. Avital Falk explained in our interview. "[People] tend to avoid those things and then it brings relief, so their bodies and brain think, 'Oh that worked for me! That was a good strategy!' And they do it more and more." The downside to avoiding things is that it actually makes your fear of them worse. Dr. Villiers, who has an incredibly high success rate treating teenagers with severe anxiety, told me, "You're not going to get over your anxiety until you start learning how to increase it, not decrease it. Knowing what situations will trigger anxiety and then seeking out those situations very deliberately in a gradual way so you don't get overwhelmed." The more you face your fear, the less scary it becomes.

The thing is, avoiding the things that scare us is much easier and feels much better than confronting them head on. Some things are fairly easy to avoid. For example, let's say you're phobic of the feeling of physical exertion. Why not just skip the gym for the millionth consecutive week? Who needs it anyway? Let's say you're phobic of flying. What's the big deal about driving for three straight days instead of taking a plane?

Sometimes people have phobias of things that are harder to avoid. While you don't *have* to get on an airplane, it's harder to promise yourself that you'll never hear a thunderstorm again or that you'll never have to have blood drawn. So in these sorts of unavoidable situations, we tend to rely on certain safety behaviors that make us feel a little less anxious and a little bit more in control. For example, let's say you are fearful of dogs—you may only feel safe going to the park if you always have a friend or parent with you. Or let's say you are anxious about crowds at the mall; to feel more secure, you check to make sure you know where all the exits are in case you need to escape. Sometimes these safety behaviors involve superstitions too (a main component of obsessive-compulsive disorder, which we'll discuss more in chapter 8). For example, you're phobic of having blood drawn, but you can do it if you are wearing your lucky shirt.

Sometimes safety behaviors involve other people accommodating our fears (as in the first example), and sometimes they involve our own bizarre strategies to reassure ourselves (as in the other examples). In either case, these kinds of safety strategies can be addictive and often get us into a bigger rut than we started in. After feeling the fantastic relief that comes from using a safety behavior, you will likely start to feel like you absolutely cannot live without it. (It's kind of like the benzodiazepine of strategies). This is not true, of course, but after years of only going to the park with your parents, it's going to be a lot harder to get over that fear and feel comfortable going without them. In this way, safety behaviors tend to negate the effects of exposure. You might successfully pet a dog (which you were afraid of) but then think to yourself, "The only reason it was safe to pet that dog was because my brother was with me." No, no, no! You'll only get your money's worth from that exposure therapy if you face your fears head on and ditch those safety behaviors first. Remember that idea from chapter 4 of going with the panic rather than fighting against it? Psychologist Dr. David F. Tolin sums it up as follows: "Don't relax. Don't distract. Don't try to feel better. Don't use crutches. Instead, push into the fear."[3]

Think about the ways in which you avoid facing your anxiety by relying on safety behaviors. What are the things you do to reassure yourself (or have others reassure you) when you're in an anxiety-inducing situation? Can you push yourself not to rely on those things? Remember, the thing you fear is not inherently as dangerous as you think it is (otherwise, no one would own dogs or fly in airplanes!) so you don't actually *need* those safety behaviors. It is your sneaky brain tricking you and telling you that you do.

Medication

Many people find medication to be helpful in treating specific phobias. As with generalized anxiety disorder, some people use an antidepressant medication such as an

Julie's Story, Part 2: The Treatment That Worked

As her fear of bedbugs increasingly began to hinder her life and after much encouragement from her sister, Julie finally decided to seek out help. "Is this how you want to be when you are sixty?" her sister challenged her. "A crazy person looking for bugs?" After some false starts (Julie said her first therapist was an old man who would sometimes fall asleep when she was talking), Julie found a therapist she felt a good connection with. She also began taking medication and found that Luvox—an SSRI—helped to calm her anxiety tremendously.

In therapy, Julie's therapist worked with her predominantly on cognitive restructuring. Julie kept a journal and completed worksheets, which helped her examine her thoughts and her anxious or negative self-talk. What *were* her deepest fears about bedbugs anyway? What was the worst-case scenario? Julie not only worried that there *were* bedbugs; she also feared that she'd never be able to get rid of them, that no one would come to her house because of them, and that she'd be socially ostracized. Julie learned to combat each anxious or negative thought with a counterstatement that was more neutral or positive. Her therapist gave her the following example: "Instead of saying 'I am not going to check between my couch cushions for bedbugs' try 'I am confident and calm about sitting on this couch.'"

Julie felt that therapy was a big wakeup call to how irrational her thinking had become. "No one wants to be with the kind of person I have (sometimes) become," Julie wrote in her journal, "crazy and overemotional and nuts." Over time, she was able to use the tools she learned in therapy to generate more positive thoughts and self-affirmations. "I will not obsess with things that are not good for my brain activity," she journaled on a later occasion. "I will spend my time thinking about important, constructive things that I can make a difference in. I can control my thoughts. I am powerful in that way." Over time, the combination of therapy, medication, and the support of a new boyfriend served to calm Julie's bedbug fears and she found herself worrying about it less and less.

As Julie recalled her experiences, she noted, "I got so much insight into what your brain can do to your thoughts. . . . It takes a lot of work to improve yourself in difficult situations, and there are times you want to throw in the towel. But if you can find the silver lining and learn from yourself, it can be very powerful."

SSRI (selective serotonin reuptake inhibitor) or SNRI (serotonin-norepinephrine reuptake inhibitor; see more about both types in chapter 7) to reduce their overall anxiety. This is particularly helpful if your specific phobia is just one piece of your anxiety puzzle. If you also tend to worry generally, have social anxiety, or have some other combination of things (see chapter 8), then your doctor will most likely prescribe an SSRI or SNRI—Prozac, Zoloft, Cymbalta, and so on.

However, if you are someone who really just has one specific phobia and you need help with a particular situation (e.g., you must take a ten-hour flight and you are in a panic about it), your doctor may prescribe you a benzodiazepine medication (such as Xanax) just to get you through that moment. I knew one woman with a fear of flying, who tried several kinds of therapy and hypnosis before her doctor finally said, "You don't fly that much. Just take a Xanax when you do." For this woman, that was all she needed to move on with her life.

As described in chapter 4, the upside of benzodiazepines is that they really work; that panic is as good as gone. The downside to benzodiazepines is that they are a temporary fix. They work in the moment, but they don't actually fix the problem. If you take medication every time you have to fly or face a dog or whatever your fear is, you will never conquer your fear and be able to do these things *without* medication. Think about how often or how much your phobia disrupts your life and talk with your doctor about whether medication may be a helpful treatment.

Conclusion

Specific phobias are a much more targeted problem than most of the other anxiety disorders, and for that reason they are both easier to treat and easier to avoid. Phobias like a fear of flying are incredibly common and yet many people just find ways to work around them (driving somewhere, taking medication, staying local, and so on) without ever treating the phobia. However, as in Julie's case, there are times when a phobia can become a major stressor in your life, in which case treatment can be extremely helpful and relieving. Treatment for specific phobias may involve medication and/or therapy, such as exposure therapy or cognitive behavior therapy. The good news is, specific phobias are considered to be extremely treatable, so proceed with encouragement.

6

SOCIAL ANXIETY

....

Social anxiety, also called social phobia, is basically just another specific phobia, but instead of worrying about airplanes or spiders, you become incredibly anxious from social interactions. It's not that you're freaked out by other people—you're just freaked out imagining what they're thinking about *you*.

Definition and Symptoms

There are a few components to social anxiety. First, you are anxious about certain social situations—whether they involve having a conversation, performing in front of others, just being observed in a public setting, or all of the above, you are constantly imagining the worst. Will you make a total fool of yourself? Will people judge you? Then, because you are anxious about these situations, you become anxious that people will notice your anxiety symptoms (sweating, talking too much or too little, and so on), which will be totally and utterly humiliating. Now you're so anxious about all things social, you start avoiding these sorts of situations altogether, since they almost always lead to feeling terribly. On top of that, your painfully shy, avoidant behavior can come across as awkward or off-putting to other teens; in other words, all the things you do to avoid being noticed and judged (missing school, not talking to other people, and so on) can actually have the opposite effect, making people notice you in a negative way ("Why doesn't that girl talk?"). If this sort of thing has been going on for six months or more and it's causing problems in various parts of your life (school, friends, etc.), you have a diagnosable social phobia.

Dr. Steven Brodsky, a psychologist who has been treating anxious adolescents for over twenty years, told me that although social anxiety is the most common form of anxiety, it is rarely the problem that brings teenagers into his office. After all, people often tell themselves that being shy or introverted is a perfectly acceptable thing to be (it's much easier than rationalizing something like panic disorder or obsessive-compulsive disorder). And who hasn't experienced some form of social anxiety? Everyone has cringed at saying something awkward or gotten nervous at the thought of presenting in front of peers. Psychologist Dr. Tamar E. Chansky suggests that evolution may have hardwired these instincts into our brains long ago.[1] After all, we needed to be able to sense danger from other

Jayesh/DigitalVision Vectors via Getty Images

tribesmen (not just short-faced bears), so we had to be somewhat vigilant about how other people were responding to us.

So, if we all have some amount of social anxiety, when does it become a *problem*? Unlike with other anxiety disorders, the burden may be on *you* to decide that. Socially anxious teenagers are usually quite easy to live with, so it tends not to be parents who are signing their teenager up for therapy. (Very few parents will protest if their kid would rather be home instead of staying out late at parties or begging to go out with friends on a school night.) But if you're socially anxious and it's impacting your life in a bad way, it may be time to reach out for help.

As we'll talk about in chapter 8, anxiety disorders tend to go hand in hand with one another (and with other disorders), and social anxiety is no exception.

Jenna's Story

"I've always had anxiety," Jenna told me, as soon as we sat down. "From birth 'til now, everything bothered me. The littlest things bothered me. I just wouldn't enjoy anything." Now, at fifteen years old, Jenna presents as a smart, thoughtful, and determined girl; she is funny and personable, and you would never guess that social interactions ever gave her pause.

Jenna explained to me that anxiety has crept into different domains of her life over the years. As a child she was terrified of getting shots and talking to unfamiliar people. As she got older, she was afraid of taking tests or quizzes in school, of flying, of social events, and of generally being a failure. She had trouble sleeping. When her anxiety spiked, her mind would race, and she would feel nauseous and get stomach pain. Jenna felt that she couldn't enjoy anything because she was constantly worrying about what was going to happen. "I felt like I was going to explode," Jenna said, "and all these things were running through my mind. 'What am I doing later?' 'What will happen in the future?' 'Why am I anxious?' 'Can I fix it?' 'What if I fail?' 'How will this test impact the rest of my future?' 'Will I get a job?' The anxiety was awful."

Being at social events, such as parties or family gatherings, used to make Jenna particularly anxious. She found meeting new people agonizing and always worried about what they thought of her. "I didn't know what to say. I thought they were judging me every five minutes. If I said something wrong, oh gosh, I lost a friend! Even with family I'd be so nervous—I'd be shaking my leg or knee and I couldn't have a deep conversation. I just wanted to talk to them, and I wanted them to think highly of me and tell the rest of my family that I'm a good person."

Jenna's social anxiety intensified in middle school when a friend she felt close to began saying mean things to her. The other girl's critiques confirmed all of Jenna's fears about what other people thought of her, and she did not know how to handle it. "I would just run into the bathroom and cry," recalled Jenna. "I would just take it."

People with social anxiety often assume that others are judging them. *skynesher/E+ via Getty Images*

It's very common for teenagers who have obsessive-compulsive disorder or panic disorder to also have social anxiety. It may be because they have always been socially anxious or because their other issues made them feel self-conscious and isolated from others. Think of Charlie from *The Perks of Being a Wallflower*— although social anxiety seems like his main problem initially (he is a "wallflower," as the movie title suggests), it turns out that he had a whole bunch of other things going on like posttraumatic stress disorder from childhood abuse.

Regardless of how it started, social anxiety can take many forms and impact your life in negative ways, so let's discuss how to treat it. In this chapter, we'll talk about the causes of social anxiety and some variations on it (including performance anxiety), and we will hear from teenagers who have experienced it and overcome their challenges.

Treatment

Exposure Therapy

Just as with specific phobias, most treatments for social anxiety involve some kind of exposure therapy. (If you didn't read chapter 5, you should go back and take a peek at the part about exposure therapy.) In the case of social anxiety, the thing you will be getting exposed to is whatever kind of social situation you fear—whether it's meeting someone new, having a deep conversation, being in a crowd of people, or being around people who are unkind or putting you down. Just as with specific phobias, a psychologist may help you make a Hierarchy of Fears in order, from the least scary goals to the scariest goals. These are different for every person, so your hierarchy might look different than your friend's, even though you both have social anxiety.

For psychologist Dr. Dan Villiers, his first exposure therapy as a teenager involved something as simple as going out his apartment door. Then it was going to the store and buying food. Then it was talking to a stranger. Then it was talking to a friend, and so on. When I met with Dr. Villiers in his office, I would never have guessed that these things used to be a struggle for him. Not only did he speak easily and confidently with me—a stranger—he described how he frequently does interviews on radio and television. A pretty impressive feat for someone who used to struggle to say hello to a grocery store clerk. "I've had anxiety all my life and even to this day I have a Hierarchy of Fear," explained Dr. Villiers. "It looks very different than the one I had twenty years ago. . . . I remember that returning a purchased item to a store used to be at the top. Now it's giving a presentation or training that is streamed live on the Internet." Just like Dr. Villiers, you will see your hierarchy change over time, as you master situations that were previously unthinkable.

The downside to exposure therapy? If you have social anxiety, the whole idea of sitting and talking face-to-face with a therapist might raise your blood pressure. Unlike other phobias, your particular phobia directly conflicts with the idea of talk therapy. If you're miserable enough, or if things have gotten *really* bad, you might throw up your hands and force yourself into a therapist's office. If you're not there yet, you might try a self-help book or another strategy.

Psychodynamic Therapy

Although social anxiety is considered a phobia, it often feels a bit more complicated than, say, a fear of butterflies. Many teenagers I've worked with have had upsetting life experiences along the way—whether it was bullying, tough relationships with parents or siblings, or bad breakups—that kickstarted or at least contributed to their social anxiety in really unhelpful ways. For this reason, some people find a more open-ended talk therapy, or psychodynamic therapy (see chapter 7 for more info), to be more helpful than straight-up exposure therapy. For example, one guy I know had always felt uncomfortable talking to new people because he had the distinct feeling that either he was acting fake or other people were acting fake, although he couldn't put his finger on why he felt that way. This persistent feeling made it hard for him to develop close friendships and generally left him feeling uncomfortable in social situations. As it turned out, these ideas stemmed back to his childhood, since his father had always pressured him to appear more religious than he was in order to give off a certain impression to others. As a result, he felt caught between a rock and a hard place: if he let his guard down, he might disappoint his father, but if he kept up the religious facade, he felt like a phony. For this young man, psychodynamic therapy ended up being the most helpful treatment, since he was able to explore some of the deeper roots of his social discomfort, including his complicated relationship with his dad.

If, after some soul searching, you think that your social anxiety has to do with some specific relationships or experiences in your life that need to be figured out, then this kind of therapy might be a good direction to go in.

A Change of Scenery

While some people experience social anxiety across *all* settings (school, camp, social events, small groups of people, big groups of people, etc.), other teenagers find that their social anxiety is exacerbated by very particular situations—middle school cliques, mean girls at camp, bullies at school, feeling like they don't fit in somewhere, and so on. Even though these are pretty normative experiences (show me a person who got through high school without meeting anyone mean), they can still trigger some intense anxiety (especially if you're someone who was prone to anxiety in the first place). One girl told me she felt like an alien at school; basically, she was so different than the other kids she might as well have been from another planet.

However, just as certain settings can trigger anxiety, it is not unusual for teenagers to feel totally different (in a good way!) when they're in another setting. I'll admit, I used to roll my eyes when parents would have their children switch schools just to get a "fresh start." "Hello, avoidance," I'd think. "Switching schools won't make those problems go away!" And yet, I have to say, there is something to be said for fresh starts and finding different environments. The number of children I've seen do a complete 180 when they were in a new environment has been eye-opening.

"I need to find my people," one girl told me. "The kids in my class are not my people." Sure enough, although this girl was wracked with social anxiety at school, when she attended her favorite extracurricular activity, she felt totally comfortable and at ease.

Self-Talk

Even though people with social anxiety fear judgment from others, most of the time they are their own harshest judge, plagued by such thoughts as, "Everyone will see how bad you are at this," "You'll screw this up," "You'll look stupid in front of everyone," "Everyone will think you're a loser," and so on. If someone else said these things to us, we'd think they were a huge jerk (or we'd use a stronger word than *jerk*). But somehow, these harsh statements coming from our own brains are accepted as fact. For example, I used to take singing lessons but was painfully self-conscious about how I sounded. Every time I sensed a note was sharp or flat, I would wince, finally causing my vocal coach to throw up his hands. "You can't be both the singer *and* the critic at the same time!" he exclaimed. "Just be the singer." In other words, by constantly judging myself, I wasn't giving my voice a chance to just do its thing.

Figuring out how to change that script in your head can go a long way toward lessening your social anxiety. If you are doing exposure therapy, then that may happen naturally. For example, by the third time you say hi to a classmate and nothing terrible happens, your brain may slow down on the harsh commentary. But if it doesn't, you may have to actively work on changing those critiques that pop into your head and find new or alternative things to say. Think how differently you would feel if you replaced the thought of "No one's looking at me 'cause they all think I'm weird" with a thought such as "No one is looking at me 'cause they're thinking about the math test next period." It's the same reality ("No one is looking at me") but a different interpretation that doesn't put the blame on you. Try to notice the automatic critiques that pop into your head and start to challenge them with other ideas, for example, "That guy is staring at me because he thinks I'm a loser *or* there might be another reason." Just because the judgy voice in your head sounds authoritative, doesn't mean it actually knows what it's talking about.

Creating a Script

It may seem odd, but it is not uncommon for people with social anxiety to thrive in the performing arts. Why would this be? Because the scripted nature of their role takes away all the uncertainty of social interactions; in a play, all they have to do is follow the script. Look at John's story in chapter 7. He felt much more comfortable stepping into a role as someone else, than he did having day-to-day interactions as himself. He didn't have to worry about saying the wrong thing, because he had already memorized what to say.

Sometimes it's not just about changing the self-talk in your mind; it's about giving yourself a script or other tools to use in everyday life, to mitigate some of your social anxiety. Think about Chelsea, in chapter 3, who felt more secure interacting socially when she had a few topics of conversation at her fingertips. This did not completely erase her social anxiety, but it gave her more confidence to put herself out there and get the exposure she needed. For other people, simply thinking through the possibility of what they would do or say in an awkward situation makes them less likely to avoid it. For example, one girl I worked with would freeze when people spoke to her or asked her a question—a total deer in headlights—making the situation awkward and her anxiety worse. But after much practice, she was able to say things like, "Wait a minute, I have to think about that one" or "Interesting question," rather than staring blankly at the person. Using a simple script like that helped her to feel less awkward in these situations, if she needed a few minutes to think about how she was going to respond.

Likewise, let's say you *did* say something legitimately weird in conversation (we've all been there). What could you do next? The other day I was talking with someone I'd just met, asking them where they were from, where they went to school, and so on. Then two minutes later in the conversation, I said again, "And where are you from?" The person just looked at me oddly until I realized they had answered that same question not two minutes ago, and I had just spaced out. Awkward! "Oh no, she must think I'm a complete idiot," was my automatic thought.

But when these things happen (and they *will* happen), is there a script you could have at your disposal to help get things back on track? An awkward comment may make you feel like crawling into the nearest hole, but usually a simple "Wait, never mind" or "Scratch that" or "No, that was not what I meant to say; I take that back" will alleviate the situation. Making these types of changes and writing yourself helpful scripts can be hard to do on your own (our brains are stubborn!), so if you're struggling, you may want to consult a therapist to help with this sort of thing.

Self-Help Books/Workbooks

Self-help books can be a good starting point if you're not ready to dive into therapy. Sometimes reading other people's stories or completing workbooks to strengthen your coping skills can go a long way toward changing your social anxiety. The downside (which is true of all self-help books) is that it takes a crazy amount of motivation to make yourself really dig in and face your fears. It's one thing to *read* about a fear hierarchy; it's another to push yourself to leave your comfy couch and jump into an anxiety-inducing social situation. (And these books will be no help at all if you skim through them and then they gather dust on your bookshelf.) If you'd like to try it out, here is a good resource for social anxiety:

- *The Shyness and Social Anxiety Workbook for Teens: CBT and ACT Skills to Help You Build Social Confidence* by Jennifer Shannon, LMFT

Avoiding Avoidance

As we discussed in chapter 5, a big part of what keeps phobias alive and well are the accommodations or "safety behaviors" we use to avoid the things that make us anxious. If you have social anxiety, think about what your accomodations ro safety behaviors might be. Do you ask your parents not to take you to social gatherings or to excuse you from school events? Do you stare at your phone in social situations to avoid making eye contact with people? Do you tend to sit in the back of the classroom a lot or visit the water fountain every two minutes to avoid being called on?

Like all safety behaviors, these may feel incredibly relieving and helpful in the short term because they lessen that intense anxiety you're feeling. However, in the long term, they are actually just maintaining that social anxiety and making it harder for you to conquer. Think of Raj from *The Big Bang Theory*—the brilliant astrophysicist who has such strong social anxiety that he can't speak in the presence of a woman he's not related to. His avoidance techniques? Whispering what he wants to say to his friends Howard and Leonard so that they can speak in his place, or using alcohol to lessen his inhibition. These techniques fail Raj, who remains single for the majority of the show, despite his desperate wish to date attractive women. What would you do if social anxiety wasn't holding you back?

What do you do to avoid social situations that make you anxious? *Mixmike/E+ via Getty Images*

Medication

The medications that are generally prescribed for social anxiety are the same ones that are used to treat generalized anxiety (see chapter 3) and panic disorder (see chapter 4). As with specific phobias (see chapter 5), it's important to determine whether you are trying to treat social anxiety in the long term (i.e., your whole life) or for more of a one-time, high risk event (like a job interview, a big presentation, a performance, and so on). If it's more of a long-term, whole-life problem you're trying to fix, then you may benefit from some of the SSRI

Jenna's Story, Part 2: The Treatment That Worked

For Jenna, it was ultimately a combination of things that helped treat her social anxiety. When she was nine years old, she began seeing a therapist and then shortly after began taking medication—both of which have continued 'til today. "Taking medication has been amazing and life changing," said Jenna, who takes Prozac daily. "I used to not be able to sit still. I used to be so anxious I'd disrupt the class. I'd just talk and talk and I couldn't help it. I wasn't trying to frustrate the teacher. But taking this medication just helped drastically."

In therapy, Jenna learned strategies for self-talk—things she could say to herself when she felt her anxiety rising in different situations. For example, Jenna thinks to herself, "How do you calm yourself down?" if she's upset or "How will you talk to this person and tell them how you're feeling?" if she's in an uncomfortable social situation. Jenna also continually exposed herself to the very social situations she found frightening. "Doing it over and over again at family events, Bar and Bat mitzvah parties, trips with friends—it really helped," said Jenna. "As I got older, I've had a better relationship with people—I'd figure out a way to talk it out."

The combination of exposure, medication, and self-talk helped to quiet the harsh judgment that Jenna used to pass on herself. "I used to feel like, 'What's wrong with me?' Now I don't really care if people don't like me—I just forget about it and leave it alone. It's their loss," explained Jenna matter-of-factly. "Maybe they're not the right person for me or maybe they just said something by accident. It used to be that I wouldn't let it be in the past. I'd think about it all the time. . . . Now, I don't let it get to me."

(selective serotonin reuptake inhibitor) and SNRI (serotonin-norepinephrine reuptake inhibitor) medications we talked about in chapter 3, which just generally help to reduce anxiety. For example, Jenna found it extremely helpful to take Prozac, which is an SSRI. However, if it's more of a one-time high-risk social situation that you just need to get through, then your doctor may prescribe you a benzodiazepine medication (such as Xanax, Ativan, and so on) or a beta-blocker medication (such as propranolol) to take once and help you stay calm in the moment.

Professionals disagree about whether a long-term medication regimen is really necessary for treating social anxiety. Some, such as Dr. Steven Brodsky, believe that social anxiety is entirely treatable with exposure therapy and that medication should *not* be needed in the long term. Dr. Brodsky told me that "medication can be very beneficial if someone is in a crisis, such as possible school expulsion . . . or if they are too overwhelmed to do the work of therapy. However, medication provides only temporary or partial relief and has side effects; symptoms just come back when you end the medication. Exposure therapy provides permanent relief, essentially eliminating excessive social anxiety forever." Other psychologists I spoke with felt that, in some cases, medication was an important part of the treatment puzzle. Whether this is true for *you* remains to be seen, but the truth is that many, many people with social anxiety find medication to be incredibly helpful, so don't feel defeated or self-conscious if you choose to go that route.

Performance Anxiety

Performance anxiety is a common problem that is thought to be under the umbrella of social anxiety. In the fifth edition of the *Diagnostic and Statistical Manual of Mental Disorders (DSM-5)*, there is something called a "performance-only specifier" under the social anxiety section. If you suffer from performance anxiety, you would be diagnosed with social anxiety, with the specifier "performance only" along with it.

> "I saw a study that said that speaking in front of a crowd is considered the number one fear of the average person. I found that amazing. Number two was death. Death was number two?! This means to the average person, if you have to be at a funeral, you would rather be in the casket than doing the eulogy."—Jerry Seinfeld, comedian

Performance anxiety is a specific type of social anxiety. *monkeybusinessimages/istock via Getty Images*

As is true of most forms of anxiety, everyone experiences *some* amount of performance anxiety in their lives. Who hasn't gotten butterflies before a big class presentation or felt your heart pounding when you had to speak to an important person? (The time I met Michael J. Fox I was awkward and speechless—it was Marty McFly!—but that is a whole other story.) And let's face it—those people who say, "I really don't care what other people think about me" are kidding themselves.[2] We all care a little bit. For people with performance anxiety, though, the feeling is much more intense and often debilitating.

This diagnosis is for people who only get anxious in situations where they have to perform. Casual social interactions, parties, and all the other stuff we talked about in the first half of this chapter are a breeze, but ask them to give a class presentation or sing a solo in a concert, and they're suddenly a ball of anxiety. Whether it is public speaking, playing in a sports game, performing in a show, or taking a test, the fear of performing poorly and then being judged by others can leave people paralyzed with fear. Unfortunately, since you can have performance anxiety and still be a successful, high-achieving person, many people disregard the intense struggle that people with performance anxiety have. One accomplished college student described her experiences in an essay for one of her classes as follows:

It didn't occur to me that there were some kids who studied for their tests or wrote their papers and then went to sleep without worrying about it, without looking at the clock and wondering where the night went.

The first time I remember having a panic attack was in fourth grade. I didn't call it that. I didn't call it that until I was a junior in college. But when I was nine, I had the test the next day on the digestive system, and I didn't feel prepared so I burst into tears, the big back-shaking kind, with liquid coming from everywhere, eyes, nose, mouth. I don't remember what my mom said. I do remember that she came into my room later that night and took the diagrams of the stomach and intestines and the flashlight from under my blankets. I got a 103 on the test. No one worried, because when the tears dried, I was an overachiever.

As with social anxiety disorder, your parents and teachers may not be all that concerned by your performance anxiety, particularly if *they* think it is not causing any big problems in your life. However, it is entirely possible that they simply do not understand the toll it is taking on you. Kaia's story (see page 98) is one example of how performance anxiety can be both undermining and devastating.

As with a more general social anxiety disorder, the two main treatments for performance anxiety are therapy and medication. With regard to therapy, you may find either exposure therapy or psychodynamic therapy helpful. The former would include working up your own personal fear ladder until public speaking (or whatever performance situation you fear) feels as mundane as talking to your mom. The ladder would include exploring some of the roots of where your anxiety comes from; for example, maybe your parents always pressured you to perform as a child or maybe you had a really embarrassing moment at a performance when you were younger. Therapists may also use some combination of the two therapies, exploring some of the background of your anxiety, but then helping you to step out of the therapy office and practice facing your fears in the real world.

With medication use, performance anxiety often gets treated in the category of one-time, high-risk events that was mentioned before. For example, one psychiatrist I spoke with described a patient who is a professional trumpet player with performance anxiety. The patient has a concert about once a month and simply takes a Xanax before each performance. Many people use this same approach for big events (I've had more than one patient tell me that they took Xanax before their wedding), although this approach should be used with caution since you never know how your body will respond to a new medication. In other words, I wouldn't try taking your first Xanax right before the SAT.

Motivation can be a big factor in treating performance anxiety, since you may not feel that motivated to fix it, unless it is having a big or ongoing negative

Kaia's Story

Kaia was a high-achieving high school student, who had always considered herself smart and capable. It wasn't until she switched schools in eleventh grade that she hit what would become a major roadblock: test anxiety. Her English teacher, who was concerned that the students in the class weren't doing the assigned reading, began to give daily reading quizzes to check for comprehension. Despite the fact that she was doing the reading, participated in class discussions, and wrote thoughtful and comprehensive essays on the subject, Kaia failed quiz after quiz. "No one could understand why this was happening to me," said Kaia. "I didn't understand either. I didn't know why I was failing these quizzes, but I felt horribly about myself. I'm a really smart person—I'd never done so badly on something."

The school guidance counselor suggested she take the quizzes in a separate room. It didn't help. Kaia would shake and sweat, her heart racing, and would often end up leaving the paper blank. With the SAT fast approaching, Kaia sought out accommodations but was told that she could not receive any kind of support because she was getting good grades in school. "They were like 'You don't qualify for anything, let's just figure out coping strategies,'" explained Kaia, which felt all the more confusing for her. "I was very confused about how I had always been 'the smart one' and now was 'the dumb one.' Why was I the dumb one? Why would taking an exam make me feel dumb? Why? None of it made sense to me."

As the SAT approached, her anxiety worsened. "I was up the whole night before feeling sick," Kaia told me. "My stomach hurt, I was shaking and crying to my parents. I was like, 'I can't do it, I'm not even going to go!' [I was] terrified about doing this one insignificant thing that I thought would determine my whole future."

Kaia tried everything to calm her nerves. "I tried to control my surroundings," she said. "I brought my favorite pencils. I tried to do calm things. I did yoga before. I did all the things that you do to relax, all the coping you can do . . . and then I went. It was terrible. Nothing could work. I'd look at the time ticking down and I couldn't do it. It was really crazy. Afterwards, I went out to the car and sat and cried and cried and cried." Disheartened but determined, Kaia took the SAT three more times, with similar experiences. Despite her good grades and other achievements, Kaia felt like a total failure.

impact on your life. I knew one girl who used to do competitive gymnastics but was so stressed out by the meets that she didn't even enjoy the sport anymore. When you're at that kind of crossroads, you ultimately need to decide whether being a gymnast is your dream and worth battling the anxiety for, or whether it's just a hobby and it might be time to move on (ultimately, this girl decided it was just not worth it and she pursued other interests). Likewise, I know many people who cringe at the idea of public speaking, but they have pretty much managed to avoid it entirely, while living very successful lives. And let's face it: if you're past elementary school, the times that you'll be mandated to perform in a concert are probably few and far between. So, is this a problem worth fixing? Ultimately, you will have to be the judge of that.

Kaia's Story, Part 2: The Treatment That Worked

Although Kaia attended therapy, which she found helpful, the turning point came from a trip she took to Arizona toward the end of her senior year of high school. Visiting her older cousin who attended New Mexico State College, Kaia was impressed by how ambitious and successful he was, despite the fact that he did not go to what she would have considered a great school.

"When I came home from that trip, I realized that there's not just one way to do things," recalled Kaia. Rather than focusing her efforts on standardized testing, Kaia took a different path—shining in her classes, extracurriculars, and college interviews—eventually getting accepted to a college she adored. To this day, she is not a good test-taker but has found ways around that, researching the things she wants to pursue and then finding ways to reach her goals. "Even now I'll still cry, but then I'll think 'You know what? I have a great life. Everything's fine. Who cares about this stupid thing!' There are so many different paths to get to what you want in life," concluded Kaia. "The advice I try to tell people is, look for other things, look for other ways to getting to what you want. Look for things you like to do. Look at life in a more qualitative versus quantitative way. I love helping people see more outside the box and that they can be successful in more creative, unique ways."

Conclusion

Although social anxiety and performance anxiety are not always the most noticeable kinds of anxiety to others, they can be extremely debilitating. Unfortunately, unless it's gotten so bad that you're missing school or refusing to leave your house (which will definitely get your parents' attention), the onus may be on *you*, the person dealing with it, to seek out help for yourself. Treatment for social anxiety and performance anxiety usually includes some kind of therapy—most often exposure therapy, although psychodynamic therapy may also be a good option, depending on the circumstances. If the idea of seeing a therapist gives you hives, you can start with a book or workbook and try some exercises on your own. Since performance anxiety is something that affects a very small window of your life (unless you're a concert pianist or a top NFL draft pick), you may have to assess how motivated you are to truly make a change. As you can see from Kaia's experience, sometimes reassessing your current goals and direction can be as helpful as trying to treat symptoms head on.

MORE ABOUT TREATMENT—WHAT HELPS ANXIETY

"Does anxiety ever go away?" a tearful teenager asked me. It's a simple question that doesn't really have a simple answer. Some mental health professionals will say yes; you should be able to drop that fear of flying like a bad habit and get on with your life! Other professionals feel that some amount of anxiety is part of who we are and particularly part of who *you* are. That is, just as some people get angry more easily, or cry more easily, you may be the type of person who is just more prone to feeling anxious. In that case, the goal of treatment is a bit different: not to eliminate your anxiety, but to make it manageable—again, so you can get on with your life already!

As you can see from the personal stories in this book, there are many, many different roads to treating anxiety: mindfulness, self-help books, medication, hobbies, you name it. For tips and strategies that are particular to certain diagnoses, you can revisit those individual chapters. In this chapter, we will go into a bit more detail about some of the recommended ways of treating *all* kinds of anxiety: therapy, medication, and a healthy lifestyle.

Part I: Therapy

If your anxiety has become a problem, it's only a matter of time before somebody suggests that you go to therapy. Truthfully, aside from medication, it is the most common treatment intervention for anxiety, and research shows that it is usually the most effective.[1]

The prospect of going to therapy can make you feel anything from excited to intimidated to horrified. Many teenagers cringe at the idea of telling their innermost embarrassing thoughts to a complete stranger (or even the idea of being

Therapy is one of the most common and effective interventions for anxiety. *SeventyFour/ istock via Getty Images*

asked to sit and talk alone with a complete stranger). Others are excited about finding someone who will understand what they're going through and not think that it's crazy or weird. There are a ton of different kinds of therapy—gestalt therapy, schema therapy, interpersonal therapy, motivational interviewing, and dialectical behavioral therapy, just to name a few. In addition, therapy can be done in groups or individually, as part of a program or on your own. For the sake of brevity, I will only discuss in more detail the two most common types of therapy: cognitive behavioral therapy and psychodynamic psychotherapy. You may hear these terms thrown around if you're investigating therapy, so it is good to have a basic understanding of what they mean. I will also discuss something called short-term intensive therapy, which is a good option if your anxiety has reached a truly debilitating level.

Cognitive Behavioral Therapy

Cognitive behavioral therapy (CBT) refers to a kind of therapy established by Dr. Aaron Beck and is considered by many to be the gold standard for treating anxiety disorders. The main idea of CBT is that distorted thinking (or cognitions) leads to problematic behaviors; in other words, our thoughts and ideas about things affect our feelings and our resulting behavior.

The Greek philosopher Epictetus said, "Men are disturbed not by things, but by the principles and notions which they form concerning things."[2] In other words, it's not the actual thing that is scary—it's how you're thinking about it. It's your perspective. This is the "cognitive" part of CBT—the lens through which we view the world. For example, let's say you just heard a dog bark loudly. Depending upon your ideas and opinions about dogs (aka your perspective), that dog's bark may be the cutest, most exuberant hello you've gotten all day, or it could be a warning signal of a pending dog attack. It all depends on your interpretation. When your cognitions or thoughts have become distorted (see chapter 1), that's where the anxiety and accompanying problematic behaviors (i.e., symptoms of panic, avoidance, safety behaviors, etc.) come in. One of the goals of CBT is to get you to challenge those cognitive distortions with more realistic thinking—this is called *cognitive restructuring* (see chapter 5); with more realistic thinking, you can respond to life's challenges with a more neutral (or even positive) lens. The Roman emperor Marcus Aurelius was quoted as saying, "Choose not to be harmed—and you won't feel harmed. Don't feel harmed—and you haven't been."[3] In other words, our experiences are shaped by our thoughts and interpretations. For example, if a common fear you have is "If I travel on an airplane, the odds are high that it will crash," this is an example of *probability overestimation* (see chapter 1). As a result, every time the plane wobbles or bumps, you will sense impending doom (as opposed to someone who does not have a fear of flying, who will completely ignore the bumps and continue binge-watching TV shows on their iPad). In CBT, a therapist would show you ways to evaluate and challenge those thoughts ("Is that really likely? Do most planes crash? What are other possible explanations for what's going on?") and then formulate alternative thoughts ("Most planes don't crash" or "People fly all the time and are fine" or "Every plane bumps a little as it goes through the clouds"). As psychologist Dr. Avital Falk explained it to me, a goal of the "cognitive" part of treatment is to make sure your thoughts are as realistic as they can be, and to gain an understanding that just because you're thinking about something does not make it a reality.

Another part of CBT involves behavior (the *B* in CBT). This will involve targeting some sort of behavior that is fueled by your anxiety that you'd like to change. Often, this will include exposure (see chapter 5) and response prevention. For example, if you have obsessive-compulsive disorder and fears of contamination, your therapist may work with you on being able to touch your shoe (exposure) without then washing your hands afterward (response prevention). If you have social anxiety and worry about being judged by others, your therapy will likely include being exposed to situations where you feel judged—for example, giving a speech in front of people or asking a silly question—to help you conquer these fears. If you have generalized anxiety and worry about not being perfect, your therapist may have you write a story about you failing a test or coming unprepared for class (see chapter 5 for more about exposure therapy). The goal of these exposures is (eventually) to bring you face-to-face with the things or ideas that scare you, which will, in turn, help you to think more realistically about them. Cognitive behavior therapists will also teach you relaxation techniques for lessening your physical symptoms, such as deep breathing or progressive muscle relaxation.

Depending on what kind of anxiety you have, the therapist may focus more on the cognitive part or more on the behavior part of treatment. For example, with generalized anxiety disorder, much of the anxiety is based on cognitive distortions, so your therapist may heavy-load the cognitive restructuring exercises. If you have a social phobia, or another kind of phobia, a big part of the treatment will be the exposure part—directly facing those specific fears.

Unlike some other kinds of therapy, CBT is manualized. This means that your therapist is structuring the therapy sessions to follow a series of steps—kind of like a teacher's lesson plan. Therefore, you won't spend the session talking about the dream you had last night or the time you felt ashamed in second grade, as you might in psychodynamic psychotherapy (see the next page). The therapist will set an agenda at the start of each session to address the things you are working on. The therapist will also assign homework between sessions, to keep you practicing those skills, whether it is relaxation, exposure, or identifying unrealistic or unhelpful thought patterns.

Does It Work?

Many times, yes it does! Out of any treatment, there seems to be the most research confirming CBT as a successful treatment for anxiety disorders in adolescents.[4] Hence, the whole gold standard thing.

What Do Critics and Supporters Say?

Critics of CBT say that by treating the presenting symptoms and not necessarily exploring where they came from, therapists are just putting a Band-Aid on a deeper wound. Sure, it might help on the surface, but chances are that deeper wound will come back as a problem later if it's not properly dealt with. Supporters of the treatment say, who knows or cares about deeper wounds? The proof is in the pudding, so if CBT makes you feel better and helps you function, what more do you need?

As with all research, it's important to remember that just because a treatment shows a significant success rate, it may or may not work for you. As psychologist

Dr. Eli Lebowitz, director of the Anxiety and Mood Disorders program at the Yale Child Study Center, told me, "CBT is really great for about half of kids." CBT is a well-established treatment so it's a great place to start, but don't get discouraged if it's not the right one for you.

Psychodynamic Psychotherapy

Psychodynamic psychotherapy refers to a kind of therapy that is based on psychoanalytic ideas and methods.[5] These ideas were originally based on the work of Sigmund Freud, who is considered to be the founder of psychoanalysis, although the field has substantially changed and advanced since then. One of the underlying premises of psychodynamic theory is that we don't consciously understand or know about certain parts of ourselves; they are entirely *unconscious*. And yet, those unconscious fears, wishes, experiences, and ideas may contribute in large part to how we feel or act, without us even realizing. In other words, the things that you can actively identify as stressors (e.g., that bad grade you got or the fight you had with your friend) may not be the whole story for why you're feeling the way you are; they are just the things you can *consciously* identify. However, they may be just the tip of the iceberg of what is actually stressing you out.

For example, let's say your friend tells you she can't hang out with you, as planned. You feel disappointed and upset and end up spending the afternoon sulking in your room. Your conscious understanding of why you're upset might be, "I'm upset because my friend ditched me." Perfectly reasonable. However, there may be more to it than that. Lurking in your unconscious may be fears about whether your friends even like you, if you're likable at all, if you'll end up alone, if you don't fit in anywhere, if your parents even wanted you, and so on. These are not things you would have said (or even thought about) if someone asked you what was wrong, because they are, well, unconscious. Some of these ideas may have to do with this specific situation, but many of them may be buried in your unconscious from earlier experiences—when you weren't invited to a birthday party in second grade, how your mom would always blame you if you and your brothers got in a fight, and so on. Deep-rooted stuff. But according to psychodynamic theory, this stuff is the most important. Once you figure all of that out in therapy, things like your friend being a flake won't even faze you.

Unlike CBT, psychodynamic psychotherapy is not necessarily a manualized treatment (although there are some versions of psychodynamically oriented therapy that are manualized); as such, psychodynamic therapy sessions tend to be unstructured and more driven by whatever the patient (you) wants to talk about. In some sessions, it may be your fear of the neighbor's dog, but in other sessions, it may be your frustration with your English teacher, or the time you broke your leg when you were nine years old, or your shyness around your new crush. How does talking about all these things help your anxiety get better? The more you talk, the more the therapist is learning about you and whatever is lurking in your unconscious—your personality, how you relate to other people, what you tend to avoid, how you think, your hopes and dreams for your life, and so on. Psychologist Dr. Larry Rosenberg told me that he explains the therapy process to his patients as "There will be two of us in the room trying to get to know one of us really well."

As the therapist gets to know you, he or she will be able to see themes and patterns occurring in your life. To an outside observer (and to the patient!), it may not seem like the topic of your neighbor's dog, your English teacher, a broken leg, and your crush have anything in common, but a good therapist will be able to tease out patterns, which you might or might not have been aware of. Do you tend to have low self-esteem and blame yourself for things that aren't your fault? Do you always self-sabotage by procrastinating? Do you continue to choose friends who are mean to you? Some patterns may be positive and help you. Some patterns may be negative and feed your stress and anxiety. Some patterns may be half and half! But the main idea behind psychotherapy is that a therapist can help you gain a greater understanding of these patterns and the unconscious ideas that might be driving them (hopefully ditching some of those less helpful ones along the way).

In sum, unlike CBT, which attempts to target more specific symptoms that you, the patient, identify (e.g., social anxiety), psychodynamic psychotherapy attempts to dig beneath the surface and figure out what's in the rest of that iceberg—what unconscious ideas and experiences may be contributing to that anxiety which you didn't even realize. "When I start therapy, the symptoms are a complete puzzle," psychologist Dr. Daniel Gensler told me, "and I love mysteries. I'm hunting for clues and evidence to try to figure out the mystery. . . . I'm setting myself up as a co-investigator."

It is this process of therapy-enabled self-reflection and self-discovery that can help you to reach whatever goals your anxiety is holding you back from—whether that includes higher self-esteem, better friendships or romantic relationships, being able to tolerate uncertainty in life, and so on.[6] "The antidote to anxiety is feeling safe, feeling in charge and feeling satisfied in some way," psychotherapist Patricia Schell Kuhlman told me. "So we're trying to help you get a clear vision of your strengths, a clear vision of your challenges and ways to engage with these fears in a new way."

Does It Work?

There's a great deal of research that supports the efficacy of psychodynamic therapy.[7] One analysis of research findings determined that long-term psychodynamic therapy was not only beneficial, but that the positive effects of it kept increasing over time (after the person wasn't even in therapy anymore). In other words, when researchers evaluated people who were two years post-therapy, they showed even more improvement! Why would that be? Because therapy isn't about a therapist fixing your problems in his office; it's about *you*, the patient, learning how to think things through—first with the help of your therapist, but then on your own. So, when you leave therapy, you take those skills (and your therapist's voice in your head) with you, and you can continually improve things for yourself.

What Do Critics and Supporters Say?

Since it is less focused on immediate symptom reduction, critics of psychodynamic psychotherapy feel that it is too loosey-goosey to be reliable. If you're just chitchatting with your therapist for weeks on end, how can you tell if you're making progress? How can you tell if therapy is helping your anxiety any more than just talking to your best friend would be?

Supporters of the treatment say that it can have much deeper and more lasting effects than other kinds of therapy. It's not just about making you less anxious—it's about figuring out the whole puzzle of *you* to make your life all around better.

Common Threads of Therapies

Although CBT and psychodynamic psychotherapy came from different schools of thought, therapists today often use elements of both and may not be as dogmatically rigid as therapists in the past. Many mental health professionals I spoke with reported being "integrative" in their work, meaning that they integrate elements of different kinds of therapy; for example, they may use relaxation techniques (from CBT) but also explore the person's past experiences that may have contributed to the anxiety (a more psychodynamic approach). Dr. Gensler told me that he wants to lower his patients' "expectation that any one thing will work. But I'll be willing to hang in there for the long run with a kid, whether things work or don't work." In other words, it's all about helping enable change for the long haul, not about any one methodology.

Regardless of whether a therapist is using CBT, psychodynamic techniques, or some combination, there are certain things that are common across the board that you can expect from every kind of therapy.

- *Therapeutic alliance.* This refers to the relationship between the patient and the therapist, and it is very important. Research has shown that no matter what kind of therapy you're in, a good therapeutic alliance strongly

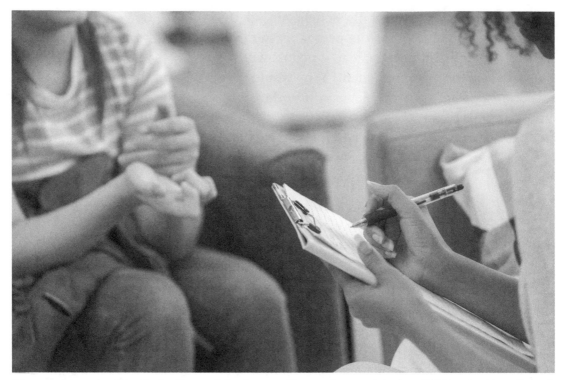

It's very important to find a therapist who you like and can relate to. *SDI Productions/istock via Getty Images*

predicts a positive outcome.[8] Therefore, it's *extremely* important that you like your therapist. (Much more so than, say, liking your eye doctor.) If you're not loving your therapist, chances are that the therapy sessions won't help you, no matter what kind of therapy the therapist is doing.

- *Psychoeducation.* As the name suggests, this refers to being educated or learning more about whatever brought you into therapy in the first place—for example, the history or prevalence of your disorder, what's happening in your brain or body, and so on. By reading this book, you've been doing a lot of good psychoeducation already, but most therapists incorporate this into therapy as well.
- *Focus on affect and expression of emotion.* Most therapists at some point will talk about feelings (such a cliché). Whether it's a "How does that make you feel?" or a "You seem angry about that," chances are you will talk a whole lot about your emotional states in therapy. Why is that? As we know, feelings play a key part in anxiety (see chapter 1), so gaining a greater understanding of them and where they're coming from will go a long way toward figuring out your anxiety and getting a handle on things. Remember the catchy phrase from chapter 3: name it to tame it!
- *Motivation to change.* How motivated you are to change can be a big factor in the success of any kind of therapy. Obviously, the more engaged and

invested in the treatment you are, the more progress you'll make! But to be honest, most people tend to be ambivalent about change. Although there's part of you that really, really wants things to be different, there's another part of you that is so freaked out by things changing that you'd be equally happy to call it a day and go back to your couch. Furthermore, there are some things about your current situation that you might actually enjoy—maybe it's not the gut-wrenching panic attacks, but things like missing school or avoiding social interactions might actually be nice perks of having anxiety that you're loathe to change. This ambivalence can result in you not giving therapy your all because, well, you're just not 100 percent on board with it. This is not unusual (no doubt your therapist will be prepared), but it certainly does not lay the groundwork for productive and effective therapy. If motivation becomes a big issue in the treatment and the therapist can sense you being noncommittal, expect that to be a topic of discussion in your next session.

Despite what you may have heard, there is no one kind of therapy that is guaranteed to work 100 percent of the time. John's story (see page 110) illustrates that different kinds of therapy can be helpful for different problems, or even at different points in your life, so don't get discouraged if it takes some time to find a therapy that's the right fit.

Therapy for Parents

Research has shown that, if therapy is not working for you, for whatever reason, it may be beneficial to have your parents try working with a therapist. Sometimes parents are doing things that maintain your anxiety or make it worse, without even realizing it, so getting them to be part of the solution may be key. Have your parents take a look at chapter 9 for a whole lot more on this.

Short-Term Intensive Therapy: When Anxiety Becomes a Crisis

Much of the anxiety discussed in this book has not reached the level that it's become a major crisis. For many people, anxiety can feel horrible and, at times, draining, but they are still able to slog through most parts of their life, using some combination of avoidance and accommodations to manage their anxiety. For others, though, anxiety can reach unmanageable levels. They cannot go to school. They cannot be alone. They cannot leave their house. In some cases, this can

John's Story and Treatment over Time

Now eighteen years old, John has had anxiety for as long as he can remember, but it hasn't always looked the same. When John was young, it was an obsessive-compulsive disorder (although OCD is no longer considered an anxiety disorder, it used to be classified as one and shares a lot of the same characteristics—see chapter 8 for more about this). Terrified by the idea of germs and getting sick, John would wash his hands "at every available moment" until they were red and raw. After using the bathroom, he would wipe himself excessively, which caused him further discomfort. "I always felt unclean somehow," John told me. He began seeing a child psychologist who used exposure therapy to help treat his OCD. During John's sessions, the therapist would encourage him to gradually be exposed to things that initially terrified him—for example, touching the bottom of his shoe and then waiting to wash his hands.

In addition to his OCD symptoms, John worried about a multitude of other scary things. "It was pretty much all the things kids are usually scared of but taken up a notch, like loved ones dying, shadows when I went to sleep at night, mummies and monsters . . . such a whole wide range of things that it's possible for a kid to be scared of," said John. "Several nights, I'd just end up crying in my bed over something that for all intents and purposes I shouldn't have been terrified of, but I just couldn't help myself." For some of these fears, John's therapist used education as a helpful intervention. For example, to address John's fear of mummies, the therapist introduced John to a book about ancient Egypt. "I always found that understanding something helps," John acknowledged. "By the time I knew more about death and all the various things I was worried about, they became much more real and not this abstract, terrifying thought in my head. I was very inquisitive, and I think that helped me to turn these abstract phantoms of my imagination into concrete realities that I could then quantify scientifically." In addition to education, the therapist also used cognitive behavioral strategies such as thought stopping, or countering "bad" thoughts with more rational ones.

By middle school, John was no longer bothered by his childhood fears, but his anxiety had morphed into a kind of social anxiety, and he became painfully conscious of what others thought about him. Unlike other people with social anxiety, John did not fear meeting new people or being thrown into social situations—in fact, he relished the opportunity to start fresh. Rather, John's fears revolved around the idea that people he knew would start to judge him or, even worse, reject him. "Am I good enough?" was the worry that kept coming back. Any kind of public humiliation was, and has continued to be, John's personal nightmare. "A lot of people wouldn't know because the outward persona that I display is very cheery, very outgoing. . . . No one would expect me to be as insecure as I am," he confided.

Today, John continues to struggle with social anxiety, but he has found several ways to cope. A talented theatrical performer, John has found his passion for theater to be a good outlet for his anxiety. "I tend to overthink things, which makes it hard for me to get into the moment," John explained, "but when I'm on stage, I can step out of my own life and not be myself. . . . I don't have to worry about what people think of me. . . . I'm just a character, interacting with other characters."

John continues to regularly see a therapist to help him with his social anxiety and he also takes medication (a selective serotonin reuptake inhibitor, or SSRI). However, just as John's anxiety has changed over the years, so has his therapy. "The kind of therapy that helped me with fears doesn't help with social interaction," John acknowledged. In his current therapy, he finds it much more helpful to have a more open-ended, discussion-based treatment. "I just find it helpful to have someone to talk to who I know will listen and understand what I'm saying and going through, and respond in a kind, gentle, and compassionate manner," John explained. "Most of our work is discussion-based and informal and that format works well here in particular."

John's story illustrates that different kinds of therapy tools—education and psychoeducation, CBT skills, a more discussion-based approach, and so on—may resonate with people at different times and for different problems; the key is finding a therapist you like, who can adapt the treatment to be most helpful to you.

result in feelings of extreme depression or suicidality. "The most extreme cases could be any disorder," explained Dr. Avital Falk, who is the director of an intensive treatment program for OCD and anxiety. "It gets to a point where the child or teenager's world has just become so small because they're avoiding anything that will trigger any sort of anxiety. . . . The more severe it gets, the more avoidance you see, and the smaller their worlds become, either because they get taken over by compulsions or by avoidance."

When anxiety reaches this level, then things need to change quickly. When you (and your family) are in crisis mode, it's not sustainable. You can't actually stay home from school forever or opt simply to never leave your house again. Something has to change fast. For some people, that means working with a psychiatrist and taking medication. For others, it may mean an intensive therapy treatment—seeing a therapist multiple times a week, or for longer periods at a time—to jumpstart getting things back on track.

Dr. Falk treats people with intense anxiety in New York City, where she leads groups for intensive short-term treatment. The groups meet multiple times a week, for several hours at a time. What do they do in those groups? The same thing someone would do if they went to once-a-week therapy for a year. They learn about anxiety (psychoeducation), they figure out their ways of thinking and identify other ways of thinking (cognitive restructuring), they do exposures to their fears (e.g., sitting in the school parking lot or maybe walking in the building), and they figure out response prevention.

"Condensing treatment can sometimes be really helpful, and for more severe or impairing cases it can be almost essential," Dr. Falk told me. "A lot of the cases I see for anxiety. . . . The reason that they're coming to do an intensive treatment program is that they have significant school avoidance or that their symptoms are so impairing that they're missing a lot of school. And if they took a year to start feeling relief, they would miss a year of school!"

But, if short-term therapy works, why wouldn't everyone just do that? Dr. Falk emphasized that short-term intensive treatment is not a substitute for strengthening those skills over time. Rather, it is an effective way to get people back to a baseline level of functioning—back in school, back at work, or whatever is needed.

"You *do* have to do it long term," Dr. Falk explained. "It's almost like in [intensive treatment], [we] are the coach or the personal trainer, and [we] are teaching people how to do all those things and getting them to a point that they feel some mastery over (a) their anxiety and (b) the skills that they need to manage their anxiety. Then they can leave with that kind of workout routine and continue it on their own . . . utilizing those skills and building those anxiety-fighting muscles." In other words, doing a short-term boot camp may help to jump start your fitness routine, but unless you keep going to the gym and strengthening those muscles, the odds of maintaining your boot camp gains over time are slim. The same is true for treating anxiety.

Conclusion: What's the Best Therapy for Me?

Unfortunately, I don't have an answer to this question. No one knows why different kinds of therapy work well for some people and do not work for others. As you can see from each person's story throughout this book, different kinds of treatment spoke to them and helped them manage their anxiety. For John, a more CBT approach was helpful initially and a more psychodynamic approach was helpful later. A particular kind of therapy may work wonders for one person but not for another. Furthermore, research has found that what kind of treatment works for you isn't even necessarily related to what kind of anxiety you have. That is, just because two people both have social phobia, they won't necessarily benefit from the same course of therapy; likewise, two people may have two different diagnoses (e.g., social phobia and generalized anxiety disorder) but both benefit from the same therapy![9] No one has a crystal ball about what will work for you; as was the case with many of the teenagers who shared their stories, it may take some trial and error before you find the right fit. The one thing I'll recommend, though, is getting into a more intensive treatment if things have really spiraled out of control. If you haven't left your couch in ten days or you're thinking about hurting yourself because things have gotten so hopeless, then you need help *fast*.

Part II: Medication

When you google "medication for . . ." *anxiety* is the first word to pop up. That just goes to show that *a lot* of people want to know more about this. Because medication is generally a controversial topic (as opposed to an intervention like "more sleep," which pretty much everyone can get on board with), you may have already developed thoughts or opinions about it. Sometimes those opinions are based on fears, such as "If I take medication, it will make me a zombie or take away my personality," or ideas like "I should be able to solve my problems without medication." Other people think medication is the best thing since sliced bread and have found it to be a real game changer—lessening their anxiety, taking the edge off, and just overall making their lives better. The number of other interventions you've tried already, and how effective they've been, may also be a factor in whether you decide to try medication. For some people, medication is their go-to; for others it's a last-ditch effort.

Research shows that medication can be very effective at treating anxiety—according to one meta-analysis, it is more effective than any other treatment.[10] If you are considering taking medication or just finding out more information about it, then the person to talk to is a psychiatrist (your regular doctor can recommend one).

Your Options

The most common medications prescribed for anxiety are antidepressants (the name of which may be confusing, since they are also used to treat depression). These medications, known as SSRIs (selective serotonin reuptake inhibitors) or SNRIs (serotonin-norepinephrine reuptake inhibitors), work by increasing certain neurotransmitters in your brain—usually serotonin, but sometimes norepinephrine too. The goal of increasing these neurotransmitters is to help stabilize your mood—that is, to take the edge off of those intense feelings you're having. Examples of SSRI medications include Prozac, Paxil, Zoloft, Lexapro, and Celexa. Examples of SNRI medications include Cymbalta and Effexor. Less commonly, doctors may prescribe other types of medications for anxiety including Tricyclic antidepressants (such as Tofranil), Atypical antidepressants (such as Wellbutrin) or Monoamine oxidase inhibitors (such as Parnate).

For more extreme anxiety, or panic attacks, a psychiatrist may prescribe a benzodiazepine medication, such as Xanax, Klonopin, Valium, and so on; these act on the central nervous system and produce sedation (that calm feeling you've been craving!). Although benzodiazepines are known for working well in the moment (great for crises!), they are highly addictive, so most psychiatrists won't prescribe them to you unless it's for a one-time use kind of thing (see chapter 4 for more about that).

With all the news out there about addiction, many people worry that they will become dependent on *any* medication (not just a benzodiazepine) if they try it. Is that true for all anxiety medication? Does starting a medication mean that you'll have to take it forever? Definitely not. Psychiatrist Dr. Simon Epstein told me that when patients ask him this, he responds, "Forever is a long time. But a few months is not a long time. So I think we should try this, get it working—there's no sense doing what *doesn't* work—and then see how you are for a month, and then we can talk about stopping it."

Conclusion: Should I Be on Medication?

Again, I'm terribly sorry, but I can't give you a definitive answer for that one either. Medication has certainly proven extremely helpful to many teenagers and young adults in your shoes; however, as we've already established, just because something is supported by research does not mean it will work for *you*. If it is something you're considering, try meeting with a psychiatrist to find out more information. And don't place too much weight on other people's opinions. I say, the proof is in the pudding, so if it helps you, great! If it doesn't, you may have to keep looking for the right intervention.

Part III: Healthy Living

Getting your anxious mind settled is no small trick. Most of the interventions we've discussed so far are focused around the brain or the mind: therapy, medication, mindfulness, and so on. Yet, any mental health professional will tell you that an equally important part of treatment should be taking care of your body. Sure, you can go to therapy, but if you're eating junk food, drinking caffeine, staying up late, and smoking pot, you're creating an uphill battle for yourself. I realize that being a teenager usually does involve some of these vices but before you indulge, it's good to educate yourself on how this may be affecting your anxiety.

Sleep

Sleep is one of those sneaky factors that we don't necessarily think is affecting us, but it actually is, in a major way. We're *all* worse off when we don't get enough sleep; we're much more likely to get emotional over something minor or totally lose it if something upsets us. If you haven't noticed this trend, pay attention the next time you sleep badly. Do you wake up the next day with the distinct feeling that the world is against you and this will just not be a good day, no matter how many lattes you drink? My husband once joked that gravity is especially strong on days when we don't get enough sleep (he said this after he dropped his toast on the floor and knocked a chair over in the span of five minutes). Of course, gravity is not really stronger—we're just a hot mess when our bodies aren't properly rested.

Countless studies have proven this to be true. Sleep loss hinders our attention, our memory, our mood, our logical reasoning, our ability to plan and make decisions—even our motor skills! (See above about dropping toast.) It's no surprise that this shutdown in functioning will take its toll on schoolwork, making sleep-deprived students' grades likely to plummet.[11]

Since we know anxiety has to do with the hormone levels in your brain (see chapter 1), and we know that sleep deprivation messes with your brain, it is no surprise that a lack of sleep (and the low-functioning state you find yourself in because of the lack of asleep) would affect your level of anxiety as well. Many people find that their anxiety tends to peak at night or the next morning if they have not gotten enough sleep. I had one girl in my office who had just become overwhelmed with anxiety in the middle of her first period class. We explored what the triggers might be until she finally just put her head down and said, "I'm so tired." She had stayed up late the night before and, as a result, had been off her game from the minute she woke up.

How much sleep *should* you be getting? Most sources say somewhere between eight and ten hours (one doctor I spoke with said that eight hours is not even enough if you are going through a growth spurt). Give your brain every fighting chance it can get to function at its strongest and best: get good sleep!

Eating Habits and Nutrition

Ever heard the term *hangry*? As in, so hungry that you're angry. Going without food is not good for our bodies and not good for our brains. And again, we don't need to give our brains any more excuses to be grumpy and reactive. Making sure you're eating throughout the day (don't forget breakfast!) can go a long way toward putting you in a calm state of mind. Even if you think you've finished growing, your body and brain are still developing, and they need fuel to do that. And make sure it's good fuel too.

It's important to be aware that *what* you're eating can affect anxiety, in addition to how much you're eating. Starbucks may seem like a good idea after a late night, but caffeine and anxiety do *not* mix. I repeat: put down the coffee. And the energy drinks. And the caffeinated soda (Coca-Cola, Diet Coke, Pepsi One, Mountain Dew, and so on). Even the iced tea. (But especially the energy drinks.) Caffeine is a stimulant, and the last thing you need is to be jumpier and have your heart racing. With anxiety, your system is already functioning in too high a gear (see chapter 1), and you don't need that fight-or-flight response exacerbated. Plus, caffeine makes it harder for you to sleep, and as we already discussed, losing sleep is not an option. "I encourage kids to avoid caffeine, as I've seen a lot of kids with high spikes in anxiety because of over-caffeination from gamer juice or monster drinks," notes Dr. Elizabeth Ortiz-Schwartz, a psychiatrist who has worked with adolescents for over twenty years. "They can really cause anxiety and panic attacks to just skyrocket." Remember, sometimes just a bodily sensation (heart racing, feeling jittery, and so on) can be a trigger for anxiety, and these are the very same bodily sensations that caffeine produces in your body. If you need to drink something hot in the morning, try herbal tea (or if it's coffee, at least make it decaf).

For some people, food and eating concerns can mingle with and become a trigger for anxiety; that is, you may worry or panic over what you ate, what you didn't eat, how you look, if you've gained or lost weight, and so on. If this sounds familiar, you should read chapter 8 about when anxiety is comorbid with eating disorders. Binge eating or restricting your eating may give you a false sense of security or control in the moment; but your body needs a healthy quantity (and quality) of food and will start to malfunction without it, making your anxiety even worse.

Substance Use

Sometimes people use drugs and alcohol to try to regulate their anxiety; teenagers have told me they feel more relaxed when they drink or smoke pot. The problem is, misuse of these substances leads to a whole host of other issues, often increasing anxiety in the process. As a result, anxiety disorders are frequently comorbid with substance abuse (see chapter 8). Remember, we're trying to get your anxious brain under control so numbing it or hyping it up with substances is not going to help. It may feel good in the short term, but it's just perpetuating things in the long term.

Exercise

Exercise may be one of those things that really speaks to you (see Kieran's connection to hockey in chapter 3). Alternately, just the thought of exercising may make you cringe. But the research on exercise has been remarkably uniform, and there are countless books, magazine articles, and infomercials about why exercise is basically the best gift we can ever give our bodies. For the purposes of this book, I'll keep it brief (and relevant to anxiety, of course).

Simply put, exercise increases blood flow in your body. This has all kinds of great benefits for your body, but one in particular is the fact that you are getting more blood flow (and oxygen) to your brain. To get technical for a minute, blood flow increases in a part of your brain called the dentate gyrus, which is a part of the hippocampus, or memory center of your brain. As a result, all kinds of brain functions—long-term memory, attention, reasoning, and problem-solving, among others—can be improved from this increased blood flow.[12] As developmental molecular biologist Dr. John Medina puts it, "To increase your thinking skills: *move.*"[13] Think how many of these brain functions play a part in your struggle with anxiety. Nothing undermines your sense of control and stability like not being able to remember things, finding it hard to focus, and struggling to solve simple problems. How much easier would it be to handle your anxiety if your brain were functioning at its best?

Of course, people exercise for different reasons—to build muscle, to lose weight, to hang out with friends at the gym, because they like playing sports or dancing, and so on. Generally, I would say all exercise is good exercise, unless you are struggling with body image and/or an eating disorder (again, see chapter 8 for more on this), in which case, excess exercise might be doing more damage than good.

Smoking

Many people with anxiety report that smoking cigarettes can create a temporary sense of calm for them. While the general rate of teenage smoking has declined over time, a considerable number of teenagers still partake. In a recent study, nearly one in five high school students (19.6 percent) reported having used tobacco products (cigarettes, cigars, e-cigarettes, etc.) in the past month.[14] Another study noted that 3.6 percent of high school seniors reported smoking daily.[15] Moreover, research has shown that people with anxiety disorders are almost twice as likely to start smoking (and the more severe the anxiety, the more likely they are to smoke), meaning that anyone reading this book is at an increased risk.[16]

Unfortunately, the momentary lull of relaxation that smoking creates comes at a high price. Smoking causes considerable damage to your body—your lungs, heart, respiratory system, and circulation (among other things)—putting you at an increased risk of getting cancer, heart attacks, strokes, and infections. (There are some pretty scary YouTube videos that go into the gory details of this, if you want to brave finding out more.) Research has shown that smoking affects your brain as well, putting you at increased risk for issues with memory, attention, anxiety, and depression.[17] And, as a teenager or young adult, your brain is at an even higher risk for being negatively affected by nicotine (a toxic chemical in tobacco) than an adult brain would be, since the brain does not fully develop until you reach your midtwenties.[18]

"The Impact." *Artist: Liz Shavrick*

Moreover, once you start smoking, the nicotine makes it addictive, tricking your brain into smoking more and more to maintain that calm, happy feeling. Try asking anyone who's successfully quit smoking how easy that was (spoiler:

it's pretty much the hardest thing ever). If you do smoke some form of tobacco product, now is a great time to think about quitting (which should involve a conversation with your doctor) and finding other ways to curb your anxiety. Those cigarettes are only making it worse!

Vaping and Juuling

Although cigarette use is on the decline, vaping and juuling seem to be on the rise among teenagers. But what exactly is vaping? When you smoke cigarettes or cigars, you are burning tobacco leaves and then inhaling the nicotine-filled smoke, but vaping devices work a little differently. Vaping devices do not burn tobacco directly. Instead, they work by heating a liquid inside the device, which creates a vapor to be inhaled. There are lots of types of vaping devices, which include e-cigarettes, vape pens, tank systems, and e-hookahs, among others. JUULpods are the name of one kind of e-cigarette that is shaped like a USB flash drive.

In a recent study by the National Institutes of Health, one in three high school seniors reported using some kind of vaping device this year.[19] According to a recent report by the surgeon general, e-cigarettes are now the most commonly used tobacco product among American youth.[20] Why are so many teenagers jumping on this bandwagon? Many see vaping or "juuling" as a totally harmless alternative to cigarettes. All the benefits of smoking without any of the risk. "It's not like smoking because you don't get addicted and you're not inhaling all the bad stuff in smoke," one teenager told me.

Unfortunately, that's just not true. E-cigarettes were originally marketed as a healthier alternative to smoking (although the jury is still out on whether they are effective at helping people quit smoking, and they are still not considered a US Food and Drug Administration–approved aid to quit smoking).[21] But to say that something is healthier than smoking does not mean much, and it certainly doesn't mean that it's harmless. On the contrary, vaping devices are filled with a liquid that often contains nicotine (which is why it feels similar to smoking in the first place). For example, all JUULpods contain nicotine; according to the company website, there are approximately two hundred puffs worth (or the same as about twenty cigarettes) in each pod. Nicotine is addictive in any form, so just because you are vaping and not smoking cigarettes does not mean you are any less likely to get addicted.

What about the vaping devices that don't have nicotine? Many teens believe that if there's "just flavoring" in the mist they're inhaling, then it's perfectly safe. What could be wrong with flavored water? The problem with vaping flavors is it can be hard to be sure exactly what you're inhaling, and the research on some of these chemicals is not fully known yet. (And unless you know what you're looking for, reading a flavor ingredient list will leave you more confused than you started.) Although manufacturers of these products state that it is the same flavorings used in food (and therefore perfectly safe), it may be that some of the chemicals are OK to eat but not necessarily to breathe in.

The effects of inhaling these chemicals into your lungs are not always known and are potentially extremely hazardous. For example, diacetyl is a chemical that is used to make popcorn flavor. Although it is approved by the US Food and Drug Administration to eat, it can be extremely unsafe to inhale, causing a severe lung disease called bronchiolitis obliterans. (The disease was nicknamed "popcorn lung" after several employees in a popcorn plant in Missouri developed it.)[22]

In short, you should be wary of inhaling anything, even if it gives you a feeling of calm. If you already have anxiety, the last thing you need is to feel short of breath or develop a respiratory disorder. Whether it includes nicotine, chemicals, or both, your brain and body will definitely be better off without it.

Physical Conditions

In chapter 1, we discussed the physical symptoms of anxiety, which can make you worry that something is wrong with your body (for example, your heart racing can make you worry that you're going to have heart failure). Often, these physical symptoms are rooted in anxiety. However, it is important to note that these kinds of symptoms—heart racing, shortness of breath, and so on—can also be caused by a physical problem. There's a reason our brains associate these symptoms with something being wrong. Sometimes there *is* something wrong. (Remember Dr. Villier's experience evaluating teenagers in chapter 5; sometimes there's more going on physically than meets the eye.)

For example, issues with your thyroid (e.g., hyperthyroidism) can cause many of the same symptoms as anxiety—increased heart rate, feelings of jitteriness, and so on. Likewise, some people have abnormalities in their cardiac rhythms (aka their heartbeat) that may cause them to feel "heart fluttering" or palpitations. This feeling may be similar to the heart palpitations caused by anxiety but in this case, it is actually caused by the way your heart functions. Some people have a fear of choking, but that feeling may be caused by a very real physical condition called dysphagia that makes it hard for them to swallow because of problems with their throat or esophagus.

The bottom line is, it's important to make sure that everything is A-OK physically and rule out the possibility of any underlying medical concerns before assuming that all your physical symptoms are due to anxiety. One high school senior I spoke with echoed this sentiment: "People who have physical stuff need to be heard and not just told it stems from anxiety or depression. I know what anxiety looks like, and I know when I'm not feeling well because of my body."

Conclusion: Stay Physically Healthy

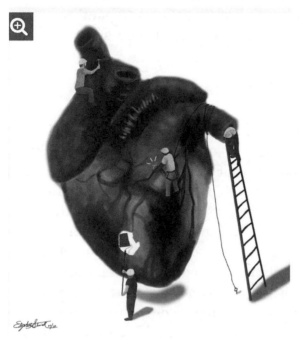

"Repairing a Broken Heart." *Artist: Liz Shavrick*

Unlike medication, this topic is not a controversial one. You'd be hard-pressed to find a medical professional who does not agree that things like sleep, exercise, and a good diet are beneficial for you, and things like smoking, drinking, and using drugs are not. Since things like coffee, smoking, staying up all night, and so on, all have an effect on your brain (and therefore, your anxiety), it is a good idea to rethink some of these lifestyle choices that may be contributing to how you're feeling. It is also important to rule out any potential physical concerns, which may present in a similar way to anxiety but have an underlying medical cause.

What *Doesn't* Work

Although there are many kinds of treatment that *do* work for anxiety (that's the whole point of this book!), research has shown, with some definitiveness, that some things do *not* work. For one thing, trying to suppress anxiety does not work. That means that if you are feeling anxious (whether it's a phobia, a social issue, or generalized anxiety), it does not help to try to ignore the anxiety or pretend that you're not experiencing it. Have you ever had a friend or parent say, "Stop worrying about it" or "Just don't think about it"? Well that doesn't work, and research studies have even proven that that doesn't work. In fact, research has shown that the harder we try *not* to think about something, the more it keeps popping into our brains, making us anxious. In one study, researchers found that when people were trying to ignore a specific thought, it made them *more* preoccupied with that thought than if they had just been allowed to think about it in the first place.[23] Famous Russian author Fyodor Dostoyevsky summarizes this problem in one of his essays: "Try to pose for yourself this task: not to think of a polar bear, and you will see that the cursed thing will come to mind every minute."[24]

This certainly holds true for anxious thoughts as well (in addition to polar bears). In one study, researchers found that when people were told to mask the anxiety they were feeling, their brains showed increased activation; in other words, by trying not to express their anxiety, people were making it worse.[25] So the next time someone tells you to just ignore your anxious thoughts or to put them out of your mind, you can tell them that, scientifically speaking, that doesn't work.

The Good News: Your Brain Can Change

One of the most discouraging things about having anxiety can be the feeling that things will never change. If you've tried two different therapies, three kinds of medications, and taken up hot yoga, but your anxiety is holding strong, this can certainly be frustrating. To give you a ray of hope, however, let's talk for a minute about your amazing brain. What scientists have shown is that the brain is constantly changing based on what kind of information it's getting. As we learn new things, the brain is making new neural connections and ditching old ones. As we relearn things, the brain is strengthening those neural connections, making it easier for us to remember them. This is not just true when you're a baby; throughout your life, your brain is continually rewiring itself as you learn new skills and have new experiences. As Medina puts it, "Like a beautiful, rigorously trained ballerina, we are hardwired to be flexible."[26]

Much of the research around this kind of brain flexibility—called *neuroplasticity*—has focused on people who have had damage to some part of their bodies or brains (e.g., stroke victims) and the amazing ways in which their brains were able to rewire themselves in order to find ways to compensate. However, recent research has begun to explore what neuroplasticity means for mental health issues; with the right training, can we rewire our brains to function better? Can we strengthen the parts of our brain that we'd like to help us in everyday life—our memory or focus or social abilities? New evidence seems to suggest that we can. For example, one study looked at whether doing meditation regularly could increase people's attention. What the study found was that after nine months, people who had practiced "present-moment focused" mindfulness (which included meditative exercises meant to calm and stabilize their minds) had actually changed their brains.[27] To get technical, people's prefrontal brain regions—which are associated with attention—had increased in cortical thickness over the nine months. In other words, the mindfulness practice had strengthened the part of their brain that would help them pay attention.

In another study, researchers looked at brain scans to see whether CBT could change the brain functions of people with psychosis. What they found was that people who participated in CBT for just six months had increased connections between important parts of their brains; to get technical, there was increased connectivity between the amygdala (the part of the brain that handles all our emotions—the good, the bad, and the anxious) and the frontal lobes (the part of the brain that we use for more rational thinking and planning). In other words, according to researcher Dr. Liam Mason, the therapy had helped people to be able to "consciously re-think immediate emotional reactions";[28] rather than just being ruled by their emotions alone, they could now apply rational problem-solving skills when they were feeling overwhelmed.

What does this mean for you and your anxiety? It means that, with the right tools, it is possible to actually change the makeup of your brain chemistry. You are not doomed! Just because you have a brain that lends itself to intense anxiety, doesn't mean it has to stay that way. You just need to find the right tool—be it therapy, meditation, medication, or something else—to strengthen different pathways in your brain.

COMORBIDITY

W hen you read a book about anxiety (like this one), it can seem like anxiety can be divided into neat little categories (each with its own chapter). That is, it can seem like generalized anxiety disorder, phobias, social anxiety, and all the rest are different problems with different solutions. However, what the real world shows us is that this is simply not the case. Life is complicated. People are complicated. So, the odds of having just one simple problem that you're dealing with are slim. More often than not, it can feel like a hodgepodge of things—maybe some social anxiety, mixed with depression and a few panic attacks thrown in. Or a fear of flying and social anxiety, along with a trauma history. "We carve things up into different disorders and we say you have two, but that's kind of us just deciding that those are two disorders," psychologist Dr. Eli Lebowitz told me. "Comorbidity within the anxiety disorders is by far the rule and not the exception. If you meet criteria for one, you probably meet criteria for one more. In our data, about 70 percent of kids who present with one anxiety disorder probably have at least one additional anxiety disorder. That has a lot to do with the way we diagnose. Because in a sense what we're diagnosing is anxiety and it's manifesting with multiple triggers or in different domains."

If you go back and read the teenagers' stories in this book, you will see that most of them have more than one issue or diagnosis. Take Jenna, in chapter 6. I included her story in the chapter on social anxiety, but she also struggled with generalized anxiety and, at times, specific phobias (flying, needles, and so on).

While some people, like Jenna, have multiple issues related to anxiety, other people suffer from the combination of an anxiety disorder and a whole separate disorder as well. They may have panic disorder and major depressive disorder. Or generalized anxiety and posttraumatic stress disorder. For example, in chapter 3, you heard from Hayley and Kieran, both of whom suffered from generalized anxiety disorder. However, Hayley also met criteria for an eating disorder, and Kieran also met criteria for major depressive disorder. When two (or more) disorders happen at the same time, it is called *comorbidity*. In this chapter we will discuss common disorders that are comorbid with anxiety—obsessive-compulsive disorder, posttraumatic stress disorder, eating disorders, substance abuse, and depression—including their definitions and how they might present. We will also hear from some young adults whose experiences do not fit neatly into a single diagnosis; rather their struggles form a more complex picture.

Obsessive-Compulsive Disorder

Although it used to be considered an anxiety disorder, the most recent diagnostic and statistical manual moved obsessive-compulsive disorder into its own category. The defining features of OCD are obsessions, which are recurrent thoughts that you can't get out of your head, and compulsions, which are repetitive behaviors that you do in response to the obsessions. It is important to note that the obsessive thoughts must be "intrusive and unwanted" and cause the person a significant amount of anxiety or distress. So, this is *not* like when you can't stop thinking about your fantasy football team, or when you spend hours on end making sure your hair looks perfect before you leave the house. It's not even like generalized anxiety disorder (see chapter 3), where your worries can feel justified—failing a class at school, for example, or worrying about whether your boyfriend will break up with you. Those are things that many people worry about. However, the thoughts that come along with OCD are usually not things that other people think about; they are bizarre or disturbing thoughts that pop into your head, and you can't stop them. For example, you keep thinking that you have touched something dirty and now you will be contaminated and contract some terrible disease. Or you keep having violent images flash through your mind—for example, you harmed a loved one or your parents were in a car crash. Pretty horrifying stuff. "Obsessions are the opposite of what a person values or believes normally, so it can be very upsetting," OCD expert Dr. Steven Brodsky told me. It is important to note that people with OCD don't actually act on these terrifying thoughts. Someone with an obsessive thought that they will hurt someone is not actually going to hurt someone, any more than someone with an obsessive thought that they've contracted a rare disease in a public bathroom actually *did* contract that disease. As with all anxiety, having the thought simply does not make it so, though our brains try to convince us otherwise.

Compulsions are the rituals or physical or mental acts that you perform to neutralize the obsessive thoughts. For example, if you worry constantly about contracting some illness from a contaminated thing you touched, you may frequently shower or wash your hands to make yourself feel better. It is important to note that compulsive behaviors are generally excessive, and are not necessarily logical antidotes to the fears.[1] For example, a person may wash their hands because they fear getting sick or contaminated (which kind of makes sense), but they also might wash their hands because they obsess about a loved one getting into a car accident (which doesn't make sense at all!). Although it is not logical, it

Intense hand washing is a common compulsion for people obsessed with thoughts of contamination. *DonNichols/istock via Getty Images*

may bring the person a sense of relief in both cases. In that way, compulsions are like the safety behaviors we talked about in chapter 5. They make you feel better in the moment, but they maintain the distressing thoughts over time. "I'm only safe because I neutralized it," you might think. "I'm not contaminated because I washed my hands six times."

Anxiety is a big part of OCD, which it is frequently comorbid with; the fifth edition of the *Diagnostic and Statistical Manual of Mental Disorders (DSM-5)* states that 76 percent of adults who have OCD also have an anxiety disorder such as panic disorder, social anxiety disorder, generalized anxiety disorder, or a specific phobia.[2] As with phobias, exposure therapy is often considered the treatment of choice for OCD (see chapter 5). Dr. Brodsky explained that one of the hallmarks of OCD is that patients are frequently seeking reassurance for the horrible things they're thinking. "Could this terrible thing actually happen?" they're perpetually asking themselves, their friends, and/or Google. "What are the odds of it happening?" For that reason, according to Dr. Brodsky, therapy must not try to convince or logically persuade people that their fears are irrational. While this sort of thought-challenging technique may be helpful with other kinds of anxiety (see CBT treatment in chapter 7), it would only undermine the treatment for someone with OCD since it would be another form of reassurance for them. Rather, with a therapist's help, the person must face her worst fears and obsessive thoughts head-on and continue to expose herself to the idea until it has lost all its power and is no longer scary. "The purpose is not to convince you that what you're worried about is wrong," explained Dr. Brodsky. "The person is engaging in self-reinforcing behavior and our job is to discover what those behaviors are and begin to reverse them."

Posttraumatic Stress Disorder

Posttraumatic stress disorder (PTSD) is the only disorder involving anxiety that requires a precipitating event. In other words, something had to happen—some event or experience—that was traumatizing. People tend to use the term *traumatizing* loosely (as in, "My Insta account got hacked and I was totally traumatized"), but true trauma is much more intense—an experience where you either fear for your life or the life of someone else, or witness or experience violence, injury, sexual assault, and so on. Following the event, you then continue to reexperience it—either having flashbacks or nightmares, which lead to significant emotional distress. People with PTSD often have trouble concentrating, sleeping, or enjoying activities, and will likely try to avoid things (be it situations, thoughts, or even feelings) that may remind them of the event. PTSD can also affect people's mood and behavior, making them more impatient, aggressive, or reckless.

Severe anxiety is often a big part of PTSD, which can also include panic attacks. One example is the main character Charlie in *The Perks of Being a Wallflower* (spoiler alert!). As a child Charlie was abused by his aunt, who then died in a car crash (how's that for trauma?). As a result, Charlie is extremely anxious; he demonstrates both social anxiety and panic attacks, and we witness him having intense flashbacks to his earlier traumatic experiences. It's hard to know if Charlie's anxiety is 100 percent caused by his trauma history or if he has an additional anxiety disorder. However, it is important to note that it *is* possible to be diagnosed with both PTSD and another anxiety disorder, particularly if your worries and fears are widespread and not just focused on memories or flashbacks of the traumatic event.

Many forms of treatment can help PTSD, most notably some kind of therapy and medication (often in combination). A major goal of the treatment of PTSD is for the person to be able to discuss the trauma itself and all the feelings and thoughts (both realistic and distorted) that came along with it.

Eating Disorders

The *DSM-5* defines an eating disorder as "a persistent disturbance of eating or eating-related behavior that results in the altered consumption or absorption

People with eating disorders often fear gaining weight and are usually displeased with the way their bodies look. *Tero Vesalainen/istock via Getty Images*

of food and that significantly impairs physical health or psychosocial functioning."[3] In other words, you've developed certain kinds of eating (or not eating) habits that are hurting both your body and your mental health. There are many kinds of eating disorders, but for the sake of brevity, we'll only discuss the most common ones here.

One common eating disorder is *anorexia nervosa*, which is when people restrict how much food they eat in order to lose a significant amount of weight. In order to be diagnosed with anorexia nervosa, you must also have a strong fear of gaining weight and a "persistent lack of recognition of the seriousness of the low body weight."[4] In other words, no matter how many people tell you that you're not at a healthy body weight, you don't believe it; you either think you look great or even that you could stand to lose more weight. I've known teenagers who were so underweight they had to be hospitalized, but when they looked in the mirror, they still thought they looked fat.

Bulimia nervosa is another common eating disorder among adolescents. This is when you have episodes of intense binge eating (that is, out of control eating of large amounts of food). Then, in order to compensate, you do something to prevent weight gain such as vomiting, using laxatives, fasting, or extreme amounts of exercise. To receive a diagnosis of bulimia nervosa, this binge-and-purge pattern needs

Hannah's Story: Anxiety, PTSD, Depression, Eating Disorder

Hannah is a thoughtful, smart, determined twenty-year-old woman, who has struggled with anxiety—among other things—for almost a decade. Initially, it was separation anxiety. When she was eleven, her parents got divorced, but not before an all-out, explosive fight that Hannah witnessed. From then on, Hannah feared for both her parents' safety, whenever she wasn't with them. When she was with her dad, she worried constantly about her mom—would she ever see her again? The same was true when she was separated from her dad. "I was terrified that someone would walk up to him and kill him on the street," Hannah told me. Gripped with anxiety, Hannah began restricting her food intake, and eventually binging and purging as well.

When she entered high school, Hannah began experiencing intense social anxiety that led to panic attacks. Her first panic attack—before her high school's weekend retreat—took her completely by surprise. "I remember I was speaking to a friend and we were talking about dinner Friday night and out of nowhere I started hyperventilating. My heart was pounding. I had no idea what was happening. I genuinely thought I might be having a heart attack." A friend of Hannah's took her to the nurse, where she sat down, shaking and crying hysterically. "I couldn't even explain the thoughts I was having," recalls Hannah. "I was just terrified."

The panic attacks continued, but Hannah began to notice that they always occurred before school trips or weekend retreats, or even during breaks between classes—namely, unstructured social times. She recognized some of the same recurring thoughts—people would think she was strange, people would think she was fat, people would judge her for what she ate. "I'd look around and see that everyone else already had friends and had people to talk to during our breaks, and I didn't. So any time there was a little bit of down time or we had a free period, I would just find myself panicking," explained Hannah. "I'd be walking around by myself and I started thinking people would look at me and think, 'Oh, she has no friends.'"

As Hannah's anxiety and depression intensified, her eating disorder worsened and she began to self-harm. The first time she lightly scratched herself with a scissors, it was meant to be a punishment for eating dessert. By the time she was sixteen, she was regularly cutting her arms, and wearing long sleeves to hide the marks. Although she saw various therapists and psychiatrists during that time, she did not open up to them, and continued to deny that she had any problems.

When Hannah was sixteen, her father found out about her cutting and demanded that she see the school psychologist. Hannah complied but was completely taken aback when the psychologist suggested that she be in a residential program—an intensive program where patients live at the treatment facility so that they can be supervised at all times. "I was confused," Hannah said, "I really didn't think it was that bad."

Despite trying several medications, Hannah's anxiety and depression intensified over the next few years, and by the time she left for college, she was in a complete panic. "As soon as my parents left, I thought, 'OK, I'm just not going to eat the entire time I'm here,'" Hannah said. For the first ten days, Hannah was too depressed to get up in the mornings and would call her parents, crying hysterically every day. "I knew things were spiraling really quickly," she said. "I immediately called my dad and said I need to go back to treatment."

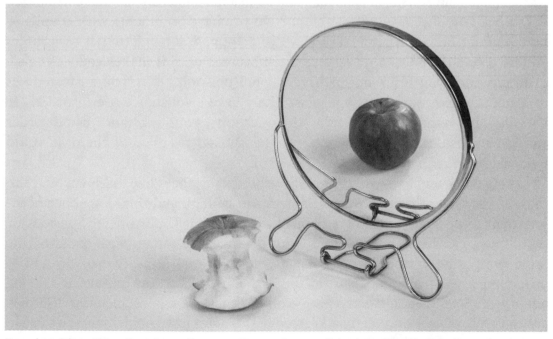

People with eating disorders often see themselves as fat when they look in the mirror, even if they're extremely underweight. *Des Green/istock via Getty Images*

to be happening at least once a week for three months. It is common for people to feel a lot of shame around binge eating, and it is most often done in private. Similarly to anorexia nervosa, people with this disorder often fear gaining weight and are usually displeased with the way their bodies look.

Both of these eating disorders usually begin in adolescence or young adulthood (I'm looking at you, reader!) and are frequently comorbid with anxiety symptoms. If you have an eating disorder and intense anxiety, it is important to find a therapist or program (depending on the severity) that can treat both right away.

Substance Use Disorders

The term *substance* can refer to any number of drugs, including marijuana, opioids, hallucinogens, stimulants (like cocaine), tobacco, or alcohol, among others. Basically, a substance use disorder is when you use, and continue to use, one (or more) of these things in excess, even though it causes major issues in your life. It's one thing to have a drink or two at a party (or even to get stone drunk at a party). It's another to drink so much regularly throughout the year that your body literally shuts down from alcohol withdrawal when you're not drinking (which makes you drink even more to avoid that withdrawal).

Do you spend a lot of your life using, recovering from, or trying to get more of the substance? Do you crave the substance when you don't have it? Have you started using more and more over time to get the same effect? Have you tried to cut back or stop but weren't able to? Do you have arguments with friends or family about how much you use? Have you stopped doing activities or hobbies you used to enjoy? Do you ever use the substance until it makes you sick (e.g., drinking until you black out or have alcohol poisoning)? If you answered yes to some of these questions, you most likely have a substance use disorder. (If you only answered yes to a few of the questions, your substance use disorder would be considered *mild*, whereas if you answered yes to all of them, it would be considered *severe*.)

Many teenagers I've worked with have used substances like marijuana to calm their anxiety; in other words, it feels better to be high and thinking about nothing, than to be sober and worrying about everything. Unfortunately, periods of withdrawal can bring anxiety back with a vengeance (along with some of the same symptoms as anxiety—restlessness, heart beating quickly, nausea, and so on), making you feel worse than you did in the first place. The teenage and young adult years (eighteen to twenty-nine years old) are when substance use disorders are most prevalent, since early adolescence is when most people first start using. As we discussed in chapter 7, your brain's best shot at truly conquering anxiety

Eliza's Story: Anxiety, Depression, Eating Disorder, Substance Abuse

Eliza, age twenty-three, is now a peer support specialist and recovery coach. When you meet her, you would never know she has a history of anxiety, let alone substance use, depression, and an eating disorder. She is thoughtful and articulate and has a good sense of humor. Her eyes twinkle as she speaks lovingly about her one-year-old daughter. For Eliza, it's been a long and difficult road to get to this point.

Raised by a single mother who herself suffered from depression, an eating disorder, and an addiction to opiates, Eliza has experienced anxiety as a way of life. "That was just my view of the world," Eliza explained. "Fear based. My mom was sick my whole life. I always had to witness scary disturbing things." By the time she started middle school, Eliza's anxiety had intensified to an unmanageable point. She worried about her friends, her weight, and her grades. As a perfectionist, she was horrified at the idea of getting a B or a C, and eventually began begging her mother not to make her go to school. She missed an increasing number of school days and then felt too embarrassed and uncomfortable to go back. As her anxiety continued to spike, Eliza began restricting her food intake and scratching at her arms. In seventh grade, she tried going away to boarding school, hoping that the change of scenery would help her. Instead she felt totally alone and experienced intense separation anxiety from her mother. After only two months, she began contemplating suicide.

By eighth grade, Eliza weighed only eighty-five pounds. "In my mind, that was a big win," noted Eliza. "I felt really proud of myself." Her friends began to express their concern, but Eliza refused to hear it, as did her mother. "Mom would say, 'We eat like birds. We eat small snacks throughout the day and that's a normal way of eating. People just don't get that because other people overeat,'" recalled Eliza. "There's nothing anyone could have said to my mom to make her realize 'Eliza has an eating disorder.' . . . Everyone was saying, 'Eliza we're so worried about you' and I would always be like, 'Don't I look nice?' and Mom would always be like, 'Yes, you look so beautiful.'"

Over the next few years, Eliza was hospitalized multiple times for suicide attempts. At times, she would reach some sense of calm in the hospital, only to have her anxiety spike again when she returned home. "I think a lot of people's experiences who are hospitalized—especially if it's an early hospitalization—is that they go, and they feel better and they feel this shift or change in their thoughts. They have more coping skills and they have a more hopeful outlook on the period of time ahead of them. They're feeling good and feeling motivated because they're also expecting everyone in their family to have gone through this kind of shift. And you come home and everything is exactly the same. And it's incredibly disheartening and infuriating." Eliza remembers feeling that any gains she had made in treatment would start to crumble as soon as she was back in the same dysfunctional family environment. Her mother was still depressed, still taking pills, and going through periods of withdrawal when she didn't have pills available. Eliza still did not want to go to school. "I missed being in the hospital. I felt really insecure in my house and that was a sad feeling," explained Eliza. "That was the first time that I realized that my life and my family was not normal and not healthy."

In an attempt to quell her anxiety, Eliza began drinking and smoking cigarettes and marijuana. By age sixteen, she was smoking daily and began having paranoid panic attacks when she was high. "I was anxious when I didn't smoke and when I did smoke, I had horrible, horrible dissociated panic attacks," recalled Eliza.

I was living in a video game and not in my body and people wanted to hurt me. I'd hear things in my house and be terrified that I was going to be murdered. . . . I felt uncomfortable around people unless I was drunk or high. I wanted people to like me but felt like nobody did like me because I was weird and annoying. My anxiety was exhausting. Really emotionally exhausting. I was depressed that I was so unhappy and depressed about my whole life. I didn't like that I cut all the time and I didn't like that I thought about food all the time. I didn't like that I stayed home and slept all day and smoked weed instead of going to school.

In eleventh grade, Eliza began raiding her mother's medicine cabinet for pills, in another attempt to self-medicate.

I had discovered that if I took an oxy [a highly addictive pain-relieving medication], I didn't care about anyone. I didn't care and I felt good about it. I could be assertive and rude—which I never felt like I could be—and also confident, and I felt good about myself. And I wasn't anxious 'cause I didn't care about anything. So, I started going to school after taking a pill and I would be able to be at school and not care. . . . I was taking huge amounts of benzo's daily because I felt like I needed it. I was just disconnected from the world, always.

Eliza's drug and alcohol use began to take its toll on her body. She was using every day and was hospitalized five times that summer for alcohol poisoning. During one incident, she was taken to the telemetry unit of a hospital (a unit to monitor patients at risk of abnormal heart activity) for a week, after she'd been drinking, taking opiates, and smoking marijuana. On another occasion, she attempted suicide by drinking and taking a lot of different pills. She started having seizures in the ICU, which the doctors could not stop. Finally, the hospital team put her in a medically induced coma. When she woke up, Eliza had suffered significant memory loss. She could not remember being suicidal, nor could she remember basic details about herself, like what kind of snacks she liked to eat or what kind of shampoo she used. "It was weeks of confusion," said Eliza. "One of the psychiatrists at the hospital told me that if I'd gotten there five minutes later, I would have been brain dead. That was terrifying and it was a turning point." By the time she left the hospital, Eliza had realized she had a problem with drugs and alcohol.

will only happen if your body is healthy too; alcohol or drugs may take the edge off in the moment, but they will only complicate things for you in the future.

As with eating disorders, there are specific programs that treat substance abuse, which can also assess whether your anxiety is just a side effect of the substance use or something altogether different. In other words, are you anxious because your body is in withdrawal or were you anxious to begin with and that's why you started using substances in the first place? Psychiatrist Dr. Elizabeth Ortiz-Schwartz told me that for patients who present with both anxiety and substance abuse, she will first treat the anxiety that comes from the withdrawal of not using. Then, once the person is no longer using, she can truly assess what their baseline anxiety is and see if it improves on its own or if it remains and requires further treatment.

Major Depressive Disorder

Depression is one of those words that gets thrown around a lot. I often hear people say "I'm so depressed!" when they're sad, or "That is so depressing!" when they hear about something upsetting. But, like anxiety, there are certain criteria that need to be met to actually receive a diagnosis of major depressive disorder (the official name for depression).

According to the *DSM-5*, you must experience depressed mood (meaning you feel sad, hopeless, discouraged, irritable, and so on) or loss of interest or enjoyment of activities every day (for most of the day) for at least two weeks. In addition to that, you must be experiencing at least four other symptoms, including

- significant weight loss or weight gain (or an increase or decrease in appetite)
- trouble falling or staying asleep or excessive sleepiness during the day
- a slowing down of thoughts or movements or a feeling of anxious restlessness
- fatigue or loss of energy
- feelings of worthlessness or excessive or inappropriate guilt
- diminished ability to think or concentrate, or indecisiveness
- recurrent thoughts of death, recurrent suicidal ideation without a specific plan or a suicide attempt or a specific plan for committing suicide[5]

As with most mental health disorders, these symptoms need to be causing significant problems in various areas of your life (social, job-related, etc.) to truly be considered a major depressive disorder. Unfortunately, depression and anxiety disorders have a high rate of comorbidity; they tend to go hand in hand. Often, teenagers can have both anxiety and depression simultaneously, but sometimes, one can lead to the other. For example, anxiety can lead to depression when a person becomes hopeless about the state of their anxiety, if they feel stuck or have not found a treatment that helped them. Types of treatment are similar for both kinds of disorders and tend to involve a combination of therapy and medication.

As we've established, people are complex, and that means that comorbid diagnoses are more common than you might think. Furthermore, what may seem like one disorder initially may morph into something quite different over time. For example, think of John in chapter 7, who was originally treated for OCD, but now fits more comfortably with a diagnosis of generalized anxiety disorder. Hannah and Eliza, the two inspiring young adults you've read about in this chapter, were kind enough to share the stories of their complicated journeys, including how they found help (Hannah's part 2 is on page 139; Eliza's is on page 140).

Stress by Eliza

Stress.
I have been stressed.
Not every day, and not all the time.
If my stress were a rock, I would be small but very dense and very heavy.
Small, rigid, bumpy, sharp, molten lava.
Bouncing around in my pocket all the time.
Some days it feels so heavy that my hips hurt and my gait is off.
Some days I forget it's there until I bump my leg against something and the rock
    digs it's ragged corner into my thigh.
And then I feel like falling over.
But I can't—and so then I become sad—no, angry.
Hot and heavy, scared and tired. My chest gets tight and my breath becomes hot
    and thick. So that it weighs down my chest, and constricts my lungs.
I feel suddenly as though I am drowning.
And then I lose it.
Maybe for a moment, because someone needs something from me.
But how dare they need me, don't they know there is molten lava in my pocket?
Of course, they don't know, it's too small to see.
Although, maybe they notice it ripping a hole in my pants, and they ask me if
    I'm ok, with a certain sincerity that rips my heart from my chest and makes
    my knees heavy. And then I just want to cry.
And then it becomes an ocean.
An ocean with huge waves and I'm stuck in quicksand being pummeled by huge
    gusts of cold, salty water.
And my eyes are red and burning, and I cannot see.
My lungs are full of salt and water, so I cannot breathe.
My mouth is full of sand and seaweed, so I have no words to say.

And I'm too scared to figure out how to move.

So like a deer in headlights, I let myself get hit by a car.

And I see it coming but cannot move or speak.

I am alone in a crowd.

A crowd of people who feel the same way as me.

But it's all a big secret, and so together we all feel alone.

Then one day I find a word—or all the words. And I find someone to tell.

Maybe they are the right person; they give me goggles, so I can see through the waves. And give me a snorkel, so I can breathe. They show me my feet and tell me how to pull myself from the thick, sticky sand.

And they cannot stay with me the whole time, but maybe they can sit with me on the shore while I catch my breath.

And then the sun can begin to rise, and the mist may clear and life begins to feel ok again.

But it always seems to cycle.

And soon again, I'm drowning.

Or maybe not always, but often enough that my knees are bruised and my elbows are scraped from falling again and again.

But I feel ok for just long enough to catch my breath.

And one day, I hope, I will have my goggles and snorkel with me always—and I won't need someone to bring it to me. My legs will be strong enough to carry my small, heavy rock. My thigh will be calloused enough so that when my molten lava hits it, I do not fall over.

Until then, I feel happy to know there are lifeguards on the shore, and that some days my rock sits quietly in my pocket and I'm able to forget that it's there.

And there are other things that make me feel strong and steady and very happy.

Like Willow.

And I'm not always perfect, and sometimes she throws my rock in my face and I melt into the ground and grow into a monster. And when the rock shrinks back into my pocket I feel so sad and guilty.

But I can hug her and say sorry.

She always seems to forgive me for being imperfect. And I'm learning how to forgive myself.

She seems to feed me a steady stream of light and love, which gives me strength and makes me feel safe and happy.

And I tell myself again and again,

"I will be ok, I will be ok."

Hannah's Story, Part 2: The Treatment That Worked

Over the past decade, Hannah has tried several kinds of treatment, including medication, individual therapy, a residential treatment program, and a partial hospitalization program (where patients can live at home but attend an intensive program at a hospital) to treat her anxiety, depression, and eating disorder. What she has found to be the most helpful is a mix of medication (Zoloft) and dialectical behavior therapy (DBT), which she now does with an individual therapist. Hannah noted that therapy has helped her realize when she's not thinking rationally and understand that those irrational thoughts are not true. For example, she remembers having pasta for dinner one night in her residential program, and then starting to cry because she worried her clothes wouldn't fit the next morning. A counselor sat with her and encouraged her to "think about this in your wise mind"; in other words, to think more rationally about the situation. Though it was a hard-earned skill, Hannah still finds it helpful to consult her "wise mind" and not her emotional one, when she is faced with situations that raise her anxiety or fill her with self-doubt.

She also uses a DBT strategy called "opposite action" in which she stops and evaluates whether the action that she wants to take makes sense. For example, when she is upset about something and feels the urge to binge and purge, she is now able to stop herself and evaluate the situation. "I tell myself, 'Right now you tell yourself that this will fix all your problems, but you know that in an hour from now when this urge passes, you're going to feel so much better about this even though you think right now you'll regret it if you don't do it,'" explained Hannah. "It has been the most difficult skill but also the most effective."

Today, Hannah feels that she's in a much better place with her anxiety. She has not had a panic attack in several years, although at times, she still feels the strain of anxiety when stressful situations arise. "It hasn't been easy," noted Hannah, "but I'm proud of myself for how I'm managing now, as opposed to how I would have managed two or three years ago. I've come very far."

One of Hannah's life goals is to be a special education teacher and destigmatize mental illness. "When I was in the depths of this, I was so angry!" Hannah remembered. "Everything was happening to me! Why did I need another thing on my plate? But now I'm kind of able to look at things like, 'there was a bigger picture here.' It's matured me so much and it's given me this incredible sense of empathy for everyone else and what everyone else is going through, 'cause I understand what it's like to suffer."

Like Eliza, Hannah's own experiences have inspired her to strive toward personal and professional goals; she wants to lead a balanced life herself, so that she can help other people get support as well. "I want to be able to be in a healthy enough place myself, in order to give my future students the teacher that they need," Hannah shared. "I want to be fully present for them. I want to be happy and I want to be helpful."

Eliza's Story, Part 2: The Treatment That Worked

After she was released from the hospital, Eliza began going to Alcoholics Anonymous meetings and began a new kind of therapy called dialectical behavior therapy (a type of cognitive behavioral therapy). She also began practicing yoga, which brought her unexpected clarity. Not knowing what it was, Eliza had walked into a Kundalini yoga class—a kind of yoga that makes you hold poses for long periods of time. Initially, Eliza was anxious about how uncomfortable she felt. "My arm started to tingle and I thought, 'I have to stop! I have to stop!' and I remember looking around and no one else was stopping. And I told myself I was going to hold it as long as I could. So, I held the pose for another thirty seconds, and I carried the feeling of that experience with me for a long time."

As is true of most people with anxiety, that feeling of physical discomfort had always been alarming to Eliza. "I need to get out," "I need to stop," "This is bad," "This needs to end," she would think to herself. "I have to get rid of this discomfort—it's going to kill me!" But her experience in yoga had made her realize that discomfort wasn't painful or dangerous. "It taught me that being uncomfortable was not going to kill me," explained Eliza. "And it helped me cope with my anxiety and my eating disorder because it made me feel strong about my body and good about my body, and that I wanted to take care of myself."

In therapy, Eliza learned several tools that she found helpful in managing her anxiety, including being aware of irrational thinking, and the cause and effect it would have on her behavior. "The most helpful thing would be actively changing the way I label something from an irrational thought to a rational thought. Or changing a 'demand' to a 'desire.' That's how I approach a lot of uncomfortable things in my life. I used to think, 'I *have* to have a cigarette right now, because if I don't have one right now, I'm going to lose it. I *need* it.' And switching that to 'I don't need it. I just want to smoke right now.'"

The road to recovery has certainly not been easy. Eliza has been on countless medications and tried every level of treatment during her life. She had one relapse with alcohol, but has now been substance free for several years and no longer smokes or takes medication. She now works as a recovery coach, who does peer support with other teenagers and young adults who are struggling. "I questioned my experiences for a long time," explained Eliza.

Why is this happening to me? This is horrible! But owning it, and telling my story, and really relating to people who are experiencing it, is an incredibly healing process. I want to tell people that I've been there and I know the feeling. I can't take it away, but I know it. At this point in my life, I still have anxiety, but I've changed my relationship with anxiety. It's not this shaming experience. . . . And now I know when I feel anxiety, it's just an experience—it's not an emergency or a disaster—it's uncomfortable. Sometimes the anxiety voice is bigger than the rational voice, but when I get out of it, I can reflect on what it was. This was a feeling—just a feeling. On this bumpy painful complicated road, I've picked up so many things along the way that have made me a person that I like to be.

Conclusion

As you can see from Eliza and Hannah's stories (and most of the other stories in this book), people's struggles with anxiety often do not fit nicely into a single diagnosis box. If this is true of you, you are certainly not alone. It is not uncommon for people's struggles to be complex, but it *can* make treatment a little more complicated than say, getting past a fear of spiders. But don't despair! Like any other problem (or combination of problems), it is just about finding the treatment that is the right fit for *you*—whether that means the right recovery program, the right therapist, the right medication, the right yoga class, and so on. No matter how many diagnoses you've been given, they all point to one thing: things in your life (and/or your brain?) have gone awry and you need help getting back on track (just like everyone else reading this book!). So take a long hard look at yourself, figure out the problems, and start asking for help.

People's challenges are often more complicated than a single diagnosis. *Bulat Silvia/istock via Getty Images*

FOR PARENTS

This chapter is for your parents or caregivers to read. They're a big part of this anxiety issue too, and if you're going to be doing all this work, they need to do some work as well. So hand it over.

Hello parents! In this chapter, we will discuss why your role is so important to your child's success, the common parenting pitfall of making accommodations, and some tips and strategies for helping your anxious child move forward. Let's get started.

Your Role (It's Important!)

What any mental health professional will tell you is that anxiety does not just happen to someone in a vacuum, especially not to teenagers. Teenagers go to school and interact with peers and live with families, and all of these things are systems that are continually shaping and affecting your child's life. *You*, parents, are a big piece of this puzzle. This is not meant to blame you for what your child is experiencing. On the contrary, the point is that you are in a uniquely well-situated place in your child's life to be able to help him or her. In fact, parents can be so instrumental in effecting change in their children's lives that many psychologists work exclusively with parents, and not with the child at all (more on this later). Why would that be?

If we think about what is at the root of anxiety, it has to do with how someone perceives danger in the world (see chapter 1)—what is safe and what is threatening. How do we, as humans, learn to do this in the first place? We learn from our caregivers. Think of when your child was a baby or a toddler. Your child looked to *you* to understand what was safe and what was not, what he should be upset about and what he could let go, what she needed help with and what she could deal with on her own. Have you ever seen a toddler fall down, look at his parents' expressions of horror, and *then* start bawling? As Dr. Eli Lebowitz and his colleagues summarize it, "Parents provide protection from threat, reassurance of safety when appropriate and aid in the regulation of inner states of arousal."[1] It's

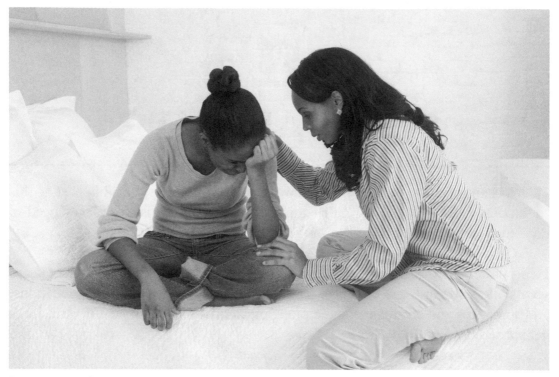

Parents can play a pivotal role in their child's struggle with anxiety. *Jupiterimages/Creatas via Getty Images*

only logical that there's a whole subset of children who are terrified to separate from their parents. How will they manage without a caregiver there to protect them? (Although separation anxiety disorder also falls under the umbrella of anxiety disorders in the *Diagnostic and Statistical Manual of Mental Disorders*, I have not included it in this book since it is most prevalent in younger children and infrequent among adolescents.)

Although adolescents' anxiety is rarely conceptualized in the same way as separation anxiety (after all, it is rare that teenagers would fear being separated from their parents), many of their fears *are* similar; for example, anxious teenagers feel vulnerable to being exposed to something dangerous, they worry that their loved ones will be at risk, and so on. As they worry, their inner states of arousal are in turmoil; the emotional parts of their brain are jumping the gun and they are reading situations as dangerous, even when they are not. This, in turn, triggers the same reactions that they had as babies; they look for help, reassurance, and protection, usually from their caregivers. I've had parents in my office who explain with shock and dismay that their fully grown teenagers will still curl up in a ball, crying and screaming, "Why won't you help me?!" when they are overwhelmed with anxiety. When we look at anxiety through this lens—the lens of *attachment theory*—it makes total sense that parents would play a huge role in helping a child (even if it's a teenage child) manage his or her anxiety.

That's fine in theory, but practically speaking, it can be extremely stressful and hard to know exactly *how* to help your anxious child. It's incredibly distressing to see your child so upset. I once heard a saying, "You're only as happy as your least happy child," which I believe 100 percent! This is the other side of attachment theory—as parents, we are hardwired to want to help and protect our children. Whether they are babies or teenagers, it is absolute torture to a parent to see your child so upset and to feel completely ineffective. Desperation to fix the situation is most parents' MO. Unfortunately, this often leads to accommodation.

Family Accommodation

Although most parents hate the idea of accommodating their children ("They're not the boss!"), studies show that we pretty much all do it. Accommodation is not always a bad thing in parenting. As every parent knows, you have to pick your battles, and sometimes that means going along with whatever harebrained scheme your child is insisting upon. Your child only wants to eat chicken nuggets three meals a day. She doesn't like getting dressed before she's eaten breakfast. He likes to listen to blasting music while he does his homework. Every parent negotiates issues like these on a regular basis and works hard to navigate their child's idiosyncrasies. Parents who make accommodations with respect to their child's anxiety are no different. It is most likely the same thought process: "How can I work around this problem so we can get on with our lives?" "When do I insist on something and when do I give in?"

Family accommodations for anxiety may include parents changing or modifying their own behaviors to reduce their child's anxiety (e.g., "If it makes you upset, I just won't go out" or "If you don't like it, we don't have to invite people over"). Accommodations may also include a parent participating in the child's anxiety-related behavior (e.g., "I know you're worried that all the doors are locked so I'll help you check them" or "Let's not go to the grocery store because I know you get nervous there").[2] In one study, researchers interviewed seventy-five parents of anxious children, and found that 97.3 percent of parents reported making at least some kind of family accommodation for their child's anxiety.[3] In other words, this is something that nearly all parents do. Start to think about the ways in which you accommodate your child. (You may think of it as "helping" not "accommodating," but as you'll see, it's not helping your child in the way that you think it is.)

As accommodations become entrenched in your family culture, your teen will feel good about it. *Really* good about it. As was mentioned in chapter 1, many people with anxiety crave control and, with the aid of some family accommodations, you have helped your child to create a contained little world in which he is able to feel in control. He can do the things he likes (even if it means washing his hands to his heart's delight or not sitting on any surface that's previously been sat on), and he can completely avoid those fear-inducing situations that get his heart racing. This may seem like a good thing: haven't you given your child a safe space, a place where he can genuinely relax? Not exactly.

As was discussed in chapter 5, accommodating worries and the behaviors related to those worries feels good for your child in the short term, but it only serves to maintain the anxiety in the long term. Even worse, it may make your child feel that the *only* place she feels comfortable is wherever she is being accommodated—namely, at home. Since your child cannot control the rest of her world—school, activities, social events—the idea of going out into that minefield of anxiety triggers will start to feel increasingly terrifying, and the idea of staying put on the couch will start to feel increasingly good. Dr. Eli Lebowitz and Dr. Chaim Omer explain it like this: "Children who can control their home environment are faced with an unhealthy choice: stay home (with less adaptive-functioning) and do not face the anxiety, or engage with the world but relinquish control. The unfortunate fact is that this is not really a choice but a trap that many children are unable to overcome independently."[4] In short, accommodating your child's anxiety is actually doing the exact opposite of what you would want. It is giving her a crutch to use, but it is not strengthening her muscles and teaching her how to walk on her own. As parents, we want to help our children, but we also want to foster independence. Think of the age-old parenting adage: "Prepare the child for the path, not the path for the child." Making accommodations is preparing the path. We want to prepare the child.

Teenagers with anxiety fear that they cannot handle stressors on their own, and by providing accommodations, we are confirming those beliefs. We are giving them relief for the moment, but we are setting them up for greater and more intense anxiety down the line. "There's a slippery slope between helping and enabling," Elise Cohen, a guidance counselor at a public middle school for twenty-six years, told me. "We often have to tell parents that. They want everything for their kids, but you have to balance between giving them everything and making them feel helpless, or making them feel supported. I know it's excruciating for parents."

Stopping Accommodations

Unfortunately, stopping accommodations is often easier said than done. Why is it so hard? First, making changes to any routine (whether it's starting or stopping something) is just hard. Think about how hard it is to change your own personal routine. How many times do people announce that they are going to start dieting

"I feel completely at a loss." If you're frustrated with the situation and unsure how to help your child, you are not the only one. *Rawpixel/istock via Getty Images*

or going to the gym regularly, only to ditch these resolutions a few weeks later? Change is hard. And changing things around for one child may affect the rest of your kids, or you or your partner, in any number of stressful ways.

Second, you may not feel like the accommodations you are giving your child are a big enough deal that they require change. "Yes, I have to walk him to the bathroom in the middle of the night, because he doesn't want to go by himself; so what? It's not a problem." Many parents I speak with wish that things were different for their child but aren't necessarily motivated enough to change anything.

Third, your anxious teenager does *not* want you to change anything—she is quite happy being accommodated! So, if you try to stop accommodating her anxiety, there will be pushback. Your child may become even more anxious or upset; she may get angry and lash out. The thought of losing her accommodations is so scary to a teenager that she will fight to not let that happen. Bear in mind that this kind of response is not the exception; it's the rule. In one study, researchers found that 85.3 percent of the parents they interviewed reported that there were negative consequences when they did not accommodate their child's symptoms.[5] This could be anything from dramatic displays of distress to the child threatening to hurt himself if the parent does not do what he asks. There can also be an emotionally manipulative component to the child's reaction, which can be absolutely gut-wrenching to parents: "Why do you refuse to help me?" "You don't love me." "If you really loved me, you wouldn't do this." If this sounds familiar to you, rest assured that you are not the only one!

These sorts of behaviors—called *coercive behaviors*—often leave parents feeling stymied. You don't want to accommodate, but you don't want to escalate the situation either. You want to support your child, but not in a way that feeds her anxiety further. Moreover, your own coping skills may be severely taxed just dealing with your child's anguish! Paula's story below is one example of a parent's struggle to help her child.

Paula's Story

Paula always thought of her daughter Kelly as having a stubborn perfectionistic streak, but it was not until Kelly started fourth grade that her need to be perfect reached unsustainable levels. Academics had always come easily to Kelly in the past, but suddenly, school was incredibly frustrating for her. Gradually, homework became a major stressor for Kelly, and she began having intense meltdowns at home. The trigger was always the same. Kelly would ask her mother for help with her homework. As her mother tried to help, Kelly would become increasingly agitated. "You don't understand!" she would insist. "That's not what I need!" Over time, her agitation turned to hysteria, and Kelly would end up curled up in a fetal position, shrieking, "I can't do this! Help me! Why won't you help me?!"

Paula could see that Kelly's distress was a result of black-and-white thinking and mind reading (see chapter 1). If things weren't perfect, it was horrible, and Kelly worried about others thinking she was wrong or different, or worst of all, stupid. "It has to be perfect and if it's not exactly as she envisions something, you can see the anxiety," explained Paula. "You can see it coming up into her body and her getting tense and anxious. I can tell her 'Kelly, take a breath' and [sometimes] she can do it and she can control it. But when it's a full-on rage, it's another story. . . . It's just growing and growing to the point of no return. And no matter what I say or do, it's past that point and it becomes a full-on tantrum."

When Kelly would throw tantrums, Paula felt completely at a loss. She tried reasoning with and cajoling Kelly—reminding her that they had been through this before and it always worked out. But after countless hours of Kelly's hysteria, Paula found herself losing patience and would often end up screaming back at her. "It just angers me," Paula explained. "When she's screaming, and it seems so irrational to me, it's really hard for me to be rational back and just keep calm. . . . She's got my blood boiling so high, that I end up reacting back. I'll scream at her, 'Go to your room! Leave us alone! Just get away from us!' It's really terrible. And then I feel really guilty afterwards."

Paula recalled a particularly trying incident, in which Kelly was throwing a tantrum and Paula, feeling overwhelmed, told Kelly that she was going to take a shower. "I needed to remove myself from the situation," Paula said. "I went into the bathroom and just sat there. I didn't actually get in the shower. And she was on the other side of the door, banging and screaming, 'Why won't you help me? Help me! Help me!' And I'm yelling at her, 'You know what you need to do! I can't help you anymore at this point. I've given you all the answers I can give you.'" At a certain point, Kelly got the message that her mother was not coming out of the bathroom and she went upstairs to calm down, but the experience left Paula shaken.

After each tantrum, Paula questioned how she had handled the situation and felt guilty for not handling it differently. Had she exacerbated Kelly's anxiety by scolding her or encouraging her to take responsibility for herself? She felt stymied as to how to help her daughter. At one point, Paula took Kelly to a therapist, but Kelly just sat there, stubbornly refusing to speak. Paula tried speaking with friends about her predicament but was not sure that they really understood what she was going through. "I talk to parents and they're like, 'Oh yeah, my son did that, my daughter did that, my kid melted down last night.' But I don't think it can possibly be the same kind of meltdown," sighed Paula. "I don't think they realize how extreme it is. . . . I just can't imagine that most kids are having the reaction that this one does."

Helping Your Child: What You Can Do

Like Paula, many parents feel completely at a loss of how to handle a child with anxiety. Often, making accommodations seems like the only way to maintain any kind of peace at home, but as we just learned, it is a bit of a deal with the devil. So what can you do instead? What does support look like, if it does not include accommodations?

What follows is a list of suggestions for where to start. Some of these you may be doing already. Some of them may not fit with your parenting MO at all and you may immediately discard them. Hopefully, many will provide food for thought and next steps.

Have Confidence in Your Child (and Don't Worry about Keeping Him or Her Safe!)

In chapter 2, we talked about how our society has shifted toward a culture of safety-ism. Research has shown that today's teens are much more concerned with their own safety and are cautious about taking risks—they are less likely to drink, go to parties, go on dates, or hang out with friends without adult supervision. In many ways, this is a good thing. Rates of drunk driving, car accidents, and teen pregnancy are down (facts that make parents everywhere rejoice!). The downside is, with less experience handling difficult situations, teenagers feel insecure and unprepared when they finally face them. Exploration and experimentation are supposed to be an integral part of adolescence; how else can you figure out who you are and what you're capable of? How can you know what kind of person you are without your parents, if you never are without your parents?

In our culture of safety-ism, it seems that teenagers tend to throw the baby out with the bathwater and avoid *all* things that come with risks—even things that aren't necessarily dangerous. In this mindset, that obnoxious boy in your child's class or that teacher who brings up controversial subjects can feel as threatening to your child as being physically assaulted. "This is the flip side of iGen's interest in safety," writes psychologist Dr. Jean Twenge, "the idea that one should be safe not just from car accidents and sexual assault, but from people who disagree with you."[6]

This culture of risk aversion may benefit the more naturally reckless teenagers; unfortunately, for those with anxiety—such as your child—it can be paralyzing. Does your anxious child really benefit from believing that he is frequently unsafe without adult supervision? Or that all her decisions require forethought and protective measures? Or that he cannot survive without safe spaces and trigger warnings? Absolutely not! To feel endangered by and incapable of navigating challenging situations is the last thing your child needs. She feels like this already.

On the contrary, your child needs the confidence to know that he can venture forward (if only with baby steps) and be all right. She needs to know that, ultimately, she *can* handle her own fear or discomfort; she *can* handle that obnoxious boy or that controversial teacher. "Their caution helps keep them safe, but it also makes them vulnerable, because everyone gets hurt eventually," explains Twenge. "Not all risks can be eliminated all the time."[7]

Unfortunately, parents in the era of safety-ism often share that same feeling that their children are fragile and in need of protection from anything that may put them at risk or cause them distress. Children are much safer now than they ever were (think back, for example, to the not-so-distant past, when seatbelts were optional, bike helmets were unheard of, and kids stayed home alone and played with BB guns, among other things). Yet many parents fear that if they are not closely monitoring their teenage children at all times, then they are not doing their due diligence as a parent. But is this really true? Or are you not giving your increasingly capable teenager enough credit?

Ask yourself, do you believe your child is capable of handling things? Even stressful or upsetting things? If you have nagging doubts, and/or an overwhelming sense that your child still really needs your help to stay safe, then you need to take a step back. Maybe you feel that way because you've been in your child's shoes and you want to shield him from negative things that you experienced. Or maybe you just feel so badly about what she's going through that you feel the strong parental urge to help her avoid distress. Either way, if you're in this mindset, you are most likely going to continue accommodating your child and sending him the implicit message that he is not strong enough to handle his fears on his own. And if you are not confident in your child, it will be infinitely harder for him to be confident in himself.

Remember: you are trying to prepare your child for the path, not the path for your child. And that means preparing your child both mentally and physically for the decisions and challenges she will face down the line. Your goal cannot be for your child to always feel safe and comfortable—not only is this impractical, but it is doing her a disservice. "By placing a protective shield over our children, we inadvertently stunt their growth and deprive them of the experiences they need to become successful and functional adults," write authors Greg Lukianoff and Jonathan Haidt.[8] Rather, the best support for your child will be a combination of both acceptance and *confidence* in his ability to stand on his own two feet.[9]

Be Validating

Although a healthy amount of confidence in your child is a very good thing, we as parents need to make sure that it does not come at the expense of invalidating our

Make sure to validate your child's experience; your support means a lot to him or her. *fizkes/ istock via Getty Images*

child's experience. It is one thing to say, "I know you can do this!" It's another to be so confident that you just brush aside your child's fears altogether: "Don't be ridiculous! That's nothing to worry about!"

Psychologists Dr. Eli Lebowitz and Dr. Chaim Omer stress that parents need to walk an incredibly fine line between pushing a child to be confident in her own abilities but, at the same time, showing their child acceptance and validation. This can be a tricky line to navigate. When your child has a complete meltdown that she can't do her math homework, do you exclaim, "But I know you can do this homework! Now get going!" or even something positive such as, "But you're good at math! This will be easy for you!"? We know that having confidence in your child's abilities is important, but if you push too hard in that direction ("I know you could get past this, if you tried"), it can also make your child feel stymied and hopeless.

If you feel that, as a parent, you tend to err on the side of more confidence and less validation, take a step back. Be your child's support. Help to hold those unbearable feelings that they're struggling with. When your child tells you that he is feeling anxious about something, don't brush it off by saying something like "Don't worry about it" or "Just relax" or "You worry too much." Accept what your child is saying and feeling. The fact is, no one *wants* to be plagued by anxiety and if your child could just relax, he most certainly would! As Karen (in chapter

4) put it, "You're telling me nothing is wrong but I'm telling you something is terribly wrong." Unfortunately, your anxious child can't just relax or not worry, and making it seem like he should be able to is both invalidating and discouraging. Your child is telling you that he needs help to be able to not worry; he cannot do it on his own right now. Wouldn't you want to be taken seriously if you were reaching out for help? As one Internet meme put it, "Never in the history of calming down has anyone calmed down by being told to calm down."[10]

It is also important to note that, by brushing aside a child's fears, you may inadvertently be strengthening the idea in her mind that this fear is real, warranted, and too scary to talk about. For example, if your child shares her worry that you will get into a car accident, your first response might be "Don't think about something so terrible!" or "Why would you think about *that*? That's horrible!" Again, these comments imply that your child (or anyone, for that matter) has control over her thoughts and is thinking these thoughts on purpose, both of which we know are not the case. This kind of response may make your child feel guilty for thinking such a thing (why couldn't she control it?) and even more anxious about her scary thought, since apparently, it was bad enough to scare you as well.

What you would want to convey to your child is just the opposite: thoughts are just thoughts (whether they are scary or not), no one can control them, and you understand why they are upsetting. Let's take the previous example: your child shares his worry that you will get into a car accident. Rather than reprimanding your child or brushing aside the fear, you might say something like, "That sounds like a very frightening thought. I understand why that was upsetting, and why you are worried about it, but just thinking about it doesn't make it more likely to happen. It's just a scary thought. It can't hurt us." In other words, you are validating your child's experience, letting him know he has not done anything wrong, and reassuring him that his thoughts are not dangerous. They cannot scare you off. You can handle your child's fears, and so can he.

Remember: Anxiety Is Not Logical

This may seem ridiculously obvious, but it is easy to forget it when you're talking to an argumentative teenager with anxiety. Let's say your daughter must triple check each lock in your house before she can go to bed but doesn't give a second thought to the lock situation when sleeping at a friend's house. Or yesterday, your son had a complete meltdown because he didn't want to go to school, and today he ate his pancakes and got in the car without a problem. It makes no sense! Unfortunately, attempting to point out that it makes no sense ("But you could do this yesterday, so why can't you do it today?!") will be totally futile; most likely, it will fall on deaf ears and may just serve to annoy your child ("You just don't get it").

Work as a Team

As we discussed, making any kind of change in your family is hard, and you're going to need all the help you can get. Make sure your partner and other people in your immediate family are on the same page, so that any interventions you try will be followed across the board. (It doesn't work if you decide to stop helping your daughter check the locks every night, only to have her enlist her grandmother's help instead.) Remember that your child is also on this same team. Even when he is kicking and screaming and hurling insults at you, your child wants the same thing that you do: to get his anxiety under control. So, you are not trying to *convince* him to change. And you are not trying to force him or out-shout him into changing. You are trying to work together to create change. You are all on the same team.

Who else should be on your child's team? Educators. You may need to advocate for your child and spend a lot of time meeting with her teachers/principal/school psychologist/counselor, but it is extremely important that everyone be on the same page. If your child's anxiety is preventing her from getting a good education (maybe she is too anxious to go to school or too anxious to take tests, etc.), speak with the educators at your child's school to determine what can be done. Depending on how severely the anxiety is affecting your child's learning (and depending on if there are other concerns as well), she may qualify for an IEP (individualized education plan) or a 504 plan, which provide special services or classroom accommodations. Examples of accommodations include preferential seating in the classroom, extended time for tests, modified tests and homework, taking tests in a separate, quiet room, regular check-ins with a school counselor or preferred teacher who your child trusts, and so on. In addition, the school may be willing to make accommodations such as giving your child word banks on tests (which can be particularly helpful if your child tends to "freeze" from anxiety when taking tests), or not requiring him to read aloud or present to the class (but rather to present privately to the teacher or demonstrate his knowledge another way), any and all of which may help to lessen your child's anxiety. Even if your child's anxiety is not something that accommodations can help with (for example, your son does fine with academic tasks but is extremely socially anxious), it is important for the school to be aware so that they can help. (The last thing a child with social anxiety needs is an uninformed teacher telling him "deal with it" when he starts to panic about something).

Don't Worry about Labels

Many parents resist getting their child help or even taking anxiety seriously because they don't want their child to be labeled. I often hear parents say things such as, "I don't want my daughter getting a label that will follow her all her life" or

"I don't want my son to be defined by this" or even "I don't want my child using a diagnosis as a crutch." I understand this discomfort with labeling your child. However, avoiding the label (or avoiding the issue altogether) will not help your child overcome her anxiety. If anxiety is holding her back, she needs help, so don't overthink the labels—get her the help she needs.

It is also important to note that many teens find labels to be incredibly validating because they are finally able to put a name to all the turmoil going on inside their heads. I often hear from teenagers that before they understood what their anxiety was, they just felt crazy, and that something was wrong with them. Knowing that the thing that is making them feel crazy has a name and is extremely common, can bring teenagers a sense of relief and normalcy (see Karen's story in chapter 4).

Educate Yourself

Just as your child has been educating himself reading this book, make sure you are educated as well. There are many good books with other strategies for helping your child. Here is one good resource but your local library will undoubtedly have others:

- *If Your Adolescent Has an Anxiety Disorder* by Edna Foa, PhD, and Linda Wasmer Andrews

Create a Stable Home Life

Stability of a child's home life is one of the greatest predictors of how a child will do at school.[11] This should not be a surprise. If *anyone* has major stressors in their life, it's going to start affecting their job performance—we know that anxiety affects our ability to learn, to concentrate, to problem-solve, to remember things, and so on—and your child's job is school. This is not to blame your family for your child's anxiety, but rather to encourage you to reexamine your home life with a fresh eye. Is there fighting in the house? Do other members of your family have health concerns (either physical or mental)? Or substance use? At times, these sorts of stressors can go overlooked (usually because families are used to them), but they may be contributing to your child's anxiety. In one family I knew, the father (whose parents had survived the Holocaust) spent most family dinners speaking intensely about how World War III was likely coming soon, which would surely mean the end of life as we know it. Although the other members of the family would not have listed this as a stressor ("That's

As you and your child educate yourselves about anxiety, create an open dialogue to discuss what you've learned. *Pollyana Ventura/istock via Getty Images*

just how he is," they explained), the father's depressing doomsday predictions began to take their toll on one of the children, who was suffering from anxiety and having panic attacks. Of course, the father was not doing this on purpose—in fact, he was scarcely aware he was doing it at all. (The whole family was quite surprised when I brought it up.)

Try to assess what, if anything, in your child's home life may be contributing to her anxiety. It may not be an easily fixable problem, but at least being aware of it will help shed some light on some of your child's triggers.

Check Your Own Emotions

Just as your child is learning to understand and be mindful of her emotions, this is a skill that you can work on as well. What happens when you get frustrated or angry or upset with your child? What thoughts pop into your mind when you see your child shut down with anxiety? "Why can't he just get over it already?" "If I don't help her, she will completely fall apart." "I could help him if he wasn't so stubborn." When a child is highly anxious, she has trouble handling her own emotions, let alone someone else's, and seeing a parent or caregiver's exasperation can be a trigger for even more intense anxiety. "It was bad enough that I never knew what was wrong with me; but when others openly wondered, I became self-conscious on top of feeling cracked," noted Jon Patrick Hatcher, author of *101 Ways to Conquer Teen Anxiety*.[12] Unfortunately, it is not uncommon for anxious teenagers and upset parents to feed off each other's distress, causing things to escalate in an unhelpful way and for the child to feel even worse about her anxiety.

Paula's story is far from unusual. Many parents I've worked with lament about teenagers who are surprisingly able to hold it together at school, and then morph into screaming banshees the minute they come home, and the most distressing part to parents is that they often find themselves doing the same thing. One minute they are trying to help their child see reason, and the next they are involved in some kind of screaming match. As you can imagine, these screaming matches do nothing to alleviate either the child's anxiety or the parent's frustration and will most likely result in pounding headaches for both. If this sounds familiar, it may be time to do some introspection about how your own emotions are mixing with your child's, and whether they are causing things to escalate. Contrary to what you are trying to accomplish (i.e., making your child less anxious), heated screaming matches will only make your child less likely to talk to you and accept help.

As was mentioned previously, anxiety often has its roots in genetics, meaning that the apple doesn't fall far from the tree. This may or may not ring true to you. Some parents tell me, "Oh yes, that's exactly what I used to do" or "She's just like her father." Other parents can only blink in confusion at symptoms that don't look familiar to anything they've experienced. If you're in the first camp, and your child's experiences are embarrassingly familiar to you, think about your own struggles with anxiety (or your partner's, or your mother's, or whoever gave your child those genes). How did you (or that other family member) handle your anxiety? What helped or didn't help you? Do you wish it had been treated differently? How do you handle your anxiety now? Gaining insight into your own journey with anxiety will be both helpful for you and helpful for your child to hear as well.

Model Healthy Habits

Just as you might be reconsidering your own emotional states, you may also want to keep an eye on what kind of life habits you are modeling for your child. How many cups of coffee do you drink? Do you smoke? Do you generally sit down to healthy breakfasts and dinners, or stand at the counter eating Pirate's Booty while you scroll through Facebook on your phone? As discussed in chapter 7, physical health can have a huge impact on mental health, and whether or not he admits it, your teenager may consciously or unconsciously be taking cues from you.

Monitor Screen Time

Telling you to monitor your child's screen time may seem contradictory, since I just finished telling you earlier in the chapter how being overprotective is not helpful in having your child stand on her own two feet. However, in this case, I think it is warranted. As discussed in chapter 2, the research on social media use paints a pretty bleak picture; increased use of screens makes kids feel more isolated, unhappy, and left out, and puts them at a higher risk for anxiety, depression, and even suicide. Many teens take their phones into bed with them, which can totally derail the possibility of quiet winding-down time and a good night's sleep. I've spoken with parents who assured me that their teens didn't use social media, only to later discover hidden Snapchat and Instagram accounts. Do yourself a favor and *monitor your child's screen time*—both the amount of time and the content. What is your teen posting and what are his friends posting? What gets talked about in the group chat? Discuss these things with your teen (if he's read chapter 2, he should have a good idea where you're coming from). If your teen argues that this is an invasion of privacy, you can remind her that nothing on the Internet is actually private. (If your child wants true privacy, she can keep a diary.) Have a no-electronics-at-bedtime rule (which goes for you too!). Your teenager may push back, but it will certainly benefit her in the long run.

Imagine the Future

This is a strategy that many therapists use with teenagers and parents alike. If you and your child are feeling stuck in the present, try to envision what you want the future to look like. Your child having more friends? Doing better in school? Enjoying more hobbies? Less fighting at home? Taking a vacation as a family? Sometimes thinking about the end goal can shed some light on the path your family needs to take to get there. What would need to change in your family to make these goals possible? What kind of support would your child (or you) need to have in place? Doing this exercise may be helpful in determining a plan to change your situation.

Remember: Different Things Work for Different Kids

This is kind of the point of the whole book. Just because a certain therapist or medication worked for your nephew that does not mean that it will work for your child. Keep in mind that anxious teenagers may feel like a failure if the strategy or therapy that they try doesn't end up working. Be mindful of this; rather than

If a particular form of treatment isn't working for your child, you may need to pivot to a new course of action. *IvelinRadkov/istock via Getty Images*

continuing to push the same intervention ("But this worked for your cousin!") or focusing on something that's not working ("Why can't you try harder at therapy?"), you may need to help your teen pivot to a new path.

Remember: Change Takes a Long Time

It is important to keep in mind that change can take time. A lot of time. Most parents (and children) want a quick fix, which is completely understandable when you feel like your child's anxiety is out of control and taking a major toll on your family. Sometimes medication can provide that quick fix; so can an intensive therapeutic treatment, like the ones described in chapter 7. However, most successful interventions take time. Whether it is cognitive behavioral, exposure, or psychodynamic therapy, it will take some time in treatment before you start to see some lasting effects. This may be hard to sit with; many parents feel the distinct urge to cut to the chase—to convince their child why she shouldn't be anxious, or to jump to the top of her fear hierarchy and get it over with. You must keep in mind, though, that you are running a marathon with your child, not a sprint. You are helping her train and exercise new muscles; so even if you do see short-term gains, you (and your child) are better off sticking with it for the long haul, to really solidify those skills. "In our work with parents of anxious children we often repeat the mantra that 'the longer route is almost always the shorter one,'" explain Dr. Eli Lebowitz and Dr. Chaim Omer. "In other words, a gradual, cautious and restrained pace leads to quicker results and improvements than an attempt to charge ahead and make rapid gains."[13] If a therapist says it will only take a few sessions to cure your child's anxiety, you should be skeptical. Rapid change *can* happen quickly (sometimes people feel a vast improvement after only one session!), but longer-term treatment is needed to maintain those gains. "It's like if you broke your arm," psychologist Dr. Cassandra D'Accordo told me. "The first thing you have to do is treat it; you get a cast and fix the immediate problem. But then you are going to need physical therapy for a while to start using it again in better ways." In order to strengthen those muscles so that the arm doesn't break again, it's going to take time. Therapy is no different. Remember, Rome wasn't built in a day.

Any Progress Is Good Progress

This goes hand in hand with the last section. In your unbearable anticipation to see your child get better, you may be frustrated when you feel like your child has taken a step backward. Maybe it seemed like things were getting better, but now her anxiety has worsened. Or maybe, no matter how many fear hierarchy steps he's completed, he still freaks out when he walks onto an airplane. It definitely can be disheartening, but it's important to keep a glass-half-full perspective of your child's progress.[14] Yes, he still freaks out walking onto an airplane, but look how he was able to watch *Air Force One* without hyperventilating. In our impatience to cut to the chase, it's easy to overlook small steps that have already been mastered, but give your child all the credit he deserves! Remember when your child was first learning to crawl or talk or read? You cheered her on every step of the way! This should be no different; she needs that cheerleading more than ever!

When Therapy Doesn't Work for Teenagers

There has been plenty written (in this book and others) about the wonderful ways in which therapy can potentially help your child (see chapter 7). Yet sometimes, for various reasons, this might not be the best course of action—either your child refuses to go to therapy, or he is too anxious to open up to a therapist so he shuts down and stares at the wall. (I've had my fair share of teenagers do this in my office; it's demoralizing for everyone involved!) Sometimes this happens because a teenager is scared of what therapy will mean—whether it will involve giving voice to the "crazy" thoughts in her head, or the possibility of having to "face her fears," which may completely terrify her. Some teenagers resist therapy because they have already tried some form of treatment in the past and felt like a failure when it didn't work. Other teenagers dig in their heels because they already have friends and family members who accommodate their anxiety, and the thought of changing that whole system sounds terrible.

There are many reasons why therapy may not work for your child right now, in which case it's time to move on to plan B. Plan B may include some other kind of treatment—medication, meditation, or pretty much anything that has the potential to calm him down—or it may include a treatment for *you*. You may be thinking, "Why should I have to go to therapy when my child is the one with the problem?" First, remember that to help your teenager change, you will need to change the system of how your family functions; and if your teenager is too shut down to engage in treatment, then you may need to kick start the whole family-system-changing-effort yourself. Working with a mental health professional, you can learn strategies for both helping your child manage his anxiety (similar to what a cognitive behavioral therapist would do) and/or strategies for changing your own accommodating behavior. The good thing about the latter is that even if your child is not cooperative (and keeps throwing you the type of coercive behavior curveballs we mentioned earlier), you still have a chance to help him by changing your role in the family system. As mentioned previously, parents often unintentionally trigger their children's anxiety, or act in some way that perpetuates it; changing *your* behavior can be an extremely effective way to change your child's behavior as well.

What to Expect from Therapy for Parents

If your child is strongly resisting therapy, you may feel like you're double crossing her by going to parenting therapy sessions yourself. Not so! If your child is paralyzed by anxiety, then she probably needs you to take the initiative. "As parents move from a stance of helplessness toward one of active leadership, they often find that their child seems almost to have been waiting for them to make that change," explain Dr. Lebowitz and Dr. Omer.[15] As we mentioned earlier, your child does not *want* to feel overwhelmed by anxiety, so if you can find ways to help him (albeit in a roundabout way), he will ultimately be much happier. (In fact, research has found that when parents participate in therapy, children who had previously refused therapy are subsequently more open to it.)[16]

After getting all the background information, the therapist can help you navigate many of the steps we talked about above—determining how you are responding to and maybe even exacerbating your child's anxiety and figuring out methods to help her in a productive way. This may include how to set boundaries effectively, how to limit or eliminate accommodations, how to target specific problem areas, and so on. Therapy may also provide a huge amount of relief and support to you, if you feel completely exasperated by the situation. Having a professional with an outside perspective can both help you see the big picture and troubleshoot when you feel stymied.

If you're still having doubts, consider the recent study by Dr. Eli Lebowitz and his colleagues at the Yale Child Study Center.[17] In the study, the researchers assigned participating families to receive cognitive behavioral therapy for the child, *or* to receive a parent-based treatment (called "supportive parenting for anxious childhood emotions"). In other words, either the children were seeing a therapist or the parents were. The end result? Children's anxiety improved equally in both conditions (not to mention parenting stress). In other words, it was as helpful for the parents to receive treatment, as it was for the kids to. So, if your child is one of those kids for whom therapy just isn't working, then this might be a better option for you.

Conclusion

Just as managing anxiety is a journey for your child, it will also be a journey for you. And, much like your child's journey, it will no doubt take some trial and error and twists and turns before you figure out the best way to handle it (although by now you've probably realized that most of parenting is trial and error!). Don't despair if you try things that don't work. That is to be expected. The best gift you can give your child is unwavering support—not accommodation, but true support—as you progress down that bumpy road together. Even if it seems like your opinion or your help is meaningless or unwanted, I can assure you, it is extremely important. You are able to play a unique and crucial role in your child's journey, to help her shift from a feeling of anxiety to a feeling of mastery, even if it is one tiny baby step at a time.

Conclusion

So where to now? This book has given you lots of information, but where do you go from here? The first thing will be to take a step back and take a long hard look at your own anxiety. How and when does it affect your life? Is it just a mild annoyance or is it causing you to tear out your hair (literally or figuratively)? What are the areas of your life that have suffered because of your anxiety? Your friends? Your school experience? Your romantic relationships? You also need to consider what will motivate you to engage in treatment. Your anxiety may be getting in the way of school, but you might not give a hoot about that. But what if it's getting in the way of your relationship with your boyfriend, and *that's* something that's really important to you? Then that will be your motivation to get the ball rolling. Think about your goals and dreams for your life; how is anxiety messing that up the most?[1]

Now picture your life as you want it to be. What would it look like without anxiety playing such a major role? Research has found that the first step to learning new skills (in multiple professions such as airline pilots, professional sports athletes, and so on) is to study a picture of what that should look like.[2] For example, basketball players study the shooting or dribbling techniques of better players so that they have a clear picture in their minds of what they are working toward. This is true for reaching any goal. How do you know what you're striving for if you don't have a clear picture in your mind of what it looks like? This may be harder than it sounds. Often, when I've asked clients to picture their life without anxiety, they draw a blank. But take some time and meditate on this question a little so that a clearer picture starts to take shape in your mind. This can be a good first step in figuring out your end goals for yourself.

As you have seen from personal accounts, there is usually more than one path to addressing your anxiety. Countless psychologists I spoke with told me that many patients came to them, already having tried a different treatment that was unsuccessful. Someone tried a cognitive behavioral therapy approach and it didn't work, but then exposure therapy did. Someone tried exposure therapy and

> "*You can't go back* and make a new start, but you can start right now and make a brand new ending."—James R. Sherman, PhD, author, *Rejection*

it didn't work, but then a more traditional, psychodynamic therapy did. What works for one person may not work for another. As with most mental health issues, there is no one-size-fits-all treatment.

As I told your parents in chapter 9, you must remember that you are running a marathon here, not a sprint. It will take a lot of little steps to reach your goal, not one big leap. So, make sure to cut yourself a little slack. As we've established, your brain can be your toughest critic, making you feel discouraged and demoralized. But push back against that anxious brain and celebrate your own successes. Every step forward is a victory! Asking for help is a victory. Heck, even reading this book was a victory. Try to be your own cheerleader, rather than your own critic. One strategy many therapists use is the question: what advice would you give a friend in the same situation? If you're the good friend I know you are, you definitely would not tell your friend how worthless and awful she is. You would help him figure things out or just give him hugs if that's what was called for. Try to be that friend to yourself—with everything you've been going through, you could use the TLC.

And if you've tried one or two or five different things and nothing has helped so far, don't get discouraged! This is no easy task you have ahead of you. You are setting out to change your habits, your lifestyle, even your brain! Dr. Frank Lawlis describes it in the following way: "It takes an extraordinary amount of effort to break through the bonds of old habits. Think of old habits as built-up scar tissue—thick, inflexible and rigid—which limits your range of motion. Your job is to slowly, carefully and deliberately break those bonds, so that you can create new, more fluid and desirable connections."[3] As I said, no easy task. And how it will happen for you will be your own unique journey—it may involve therapy, medication, meditation, sports, art, friends, family, or any number of things—and it may look the same or completely different from other people you know (or the stories in this book). The most important thing is to keep moving forward, even when that feels incredibly scary and staying put feels much more comfortable. Keep your end goals in sight and continue looking for inspiration; it will give you the strength to continue when the going gets tough. You have your work cut out for you, but I am confident you will succeed.

Notes

Introduction

1. Clark, D., & Beck, A. (2012) *The Anxiety and Worry Workbook*. New York: Guilford Press, vii.
2. Schwab, L. (2008). *The Anxiety Workbook for Teens*. Oakland, CA: Instant Help Books, v.
3. Gleason, S., & Brady, E. (2017, August 30). When Athletes Share Their Battles with Mental Illness. *USA Today*. Retrieved from https://www.usatoday.com/story/sports/2017/08/30/michael-phelps-brandon-marshall-mental-health-battles-royce-white-jerry-west/596857001/
4. Toure. (2011, April 28). Adele Opens Up About Her Inspirations, Looks and Stage Fright. *Rolling Stone*. Retrieved from https://www.rollingstone.com/music/music-news/adele-opens-up-about-her-inspirations-looks-and-stage-fright-79626/
5. Lepore, M. (2017, January 26). 15 Successful People on Their Struggles with Anxiety. Retrieved from www.levo.com/posts/15-successful-people-on-their-struggles-with-anxiety
6. Lepore, 15 Successful People.
7. Gavilanes, G. (2017, September 4). Kylie Jenner Is Terrified of Butterflies, Plus More Surprising Celebrity Phobias. *People*. Retrieved from https://www.yahoo.com/news/tyra-banks-terrified-dolphins-plus-193718530/photo-p-kendall-jenner-comes-support-photo-144908170.html
8. Spencer, A. (2016, February 9). Ashley Benson: "You Have to Become One with Your Own Body." Retrieved from www.health.com/health/article/0,,20983177,00.html
9. Kessler, R. C., Chiu, W. T., Demler, O., Merikangas, K. R., & Walters E. E. (2005). Prevalence, Severity, and Comorbidity of 12-Month DSM-IV Disorders in the National Comorbidity Survey Replication. *Archives of General Psychiatry, 62*(6) 617–627. PMID: 15939839
10. Lepore, *15 Successful People*.
11. Spencer, Ashley Benson.
12. Velasco, H. (2017, July 21). Few Student-Athletes with Mental Illness Seek Help. *USA Today*. Retrieved from www.usatoday.com/story/college/2017/07/21/few-student-athletes-with-mental-illness-seek-help/37433787/

Chapter 1

1. Chansky, T. E. (2004) *Freeing Your Child from Anxiety*. New York: Broadway Books, 59.
2. Chansky, *Freeing Your Child from Anxiety*, 72–73.
3. Yerkes, R. M., & Dodson, J. D. (1908). The Relationship of Strength of Stimulus to Rapidity of Habit Formation. *Journal of Comparative Neurology and Psychology, 18*, 459–482.
4. Medina, J. (2014). *Brain Rules: 12 Principles for Surviving and Thriving at Work, Home, and School*. Seattle, WA: Pear Press, 62.
5. Dostoyevsky, F., & Garnett, C. (1914). *Crime and Punishment*. London: Heinemann, 5–6.

6. Osbon, D. K., Ed. (1991). *Reflections on the Art of Living: A Joseph Campbell Companion*. New York: HarperPerennial, 18.

7. Chansky, *Freeing Your Child from Anxiety*, 87.

8. B. R. (2015, January 29). A Crash Course in Probability. *Economist*. Retrieved from www .economist.com/gulliver/2015/01/29/a-crash-course-in-probability

9. Locsin, A. (N.d.). Is Air Travel Safer Than Car Travel? *USA Today*. Retrieved from https:// traveltips.usatoday.com/air-travel-safer-car-travel-1581.html

10. B. R., A Crash Course in Probability.

11. Edevane, G. (2018, April 18). "Am I Going Down?" App Tries to Help Anxious Flyers by Telling Them the Odds of Plane Crash. *Newsweek*. Retrieved from https://www.google.com/ amp/s/www.newsweek.com/what-are-odds-dying-plane-crash-app-892008%3famp=1

12. Tolin, D. (2012). *Face Your Fears: A Proven Plan to Beat Anxiety, Panic, Phobias, and Obsessions*. Hoboken, NJ: John Wiley & Sons, 135.

13. Kunst, J. (2013, December 13). How to Make a Mountain out of a Molehill. *Psychology Today*. Retrieved from https://www.psychologytoday.com/us/blog/headshrinkers-guide-the -galaxy/201312/how-make-mountain-out-molehill

14. Gladwell, M. *Blink: The Power of Thinking without Thinking*. New York: Little, Brown, 2005.

15. Lebowitz, E. R., & Omer, H. (2013). *Treating Childhood and Adolescent Anxiety: A Guide for Caregivers*. Hoboken, NJ: John Wiley & Sons, 101.

16. Chansky, *Freeing Your Child from Anxiety*, 84–85.

Chapter 2

1. Twenge, J. (2017). *iGen*. New York: Atria Paperback, 96.

2. Horowitz, J. M., & Graf, N. (2019, February 20). Most US Teens See Anxiety and Depression as a Major Problem among Their Peers. Pew Research Center. Retrieved from https://www .pewsocialtrends.org/2019/02/20/most-u-s-teens-see-anxiety-and-depression-as-a-major -problem-among-their-peers/

3. Twenge, *iGen*, 76.

4. Twenge, *iGen*, 78, 89.

5. Twenge, *iGen*, 87.

6. Lukianoff, G., & Haidt, J. (2018). *The Coddling of the American Mind*. New York: Penguin Press, 99.

7. Twenge, *iGen*, 99.

8. Twenge, *iGen*, 71–72

9. Twenge, *iGen*, 89.

10. Gallen, J. (2003). *Ellen DeGeneres: Here and Now*. United States: HBO.

11. Heid, M. (2018, February 5). Is It Bad for You to Read the News Constantly? *Time*. Retrieved from https://time.com/5125894/is-reading-news-bad-for-you/

12. Dobelli, R. (2013, April 12). News Is Bad for You—and Giving Up Reading It Will Make You Happier. *Guardian*. Retrieved from https://www.theguardian.com/media/2013/apr/12/news -is-bad-rolf-dobelli

13. Medina, J. (2014). *Brain Rules: 12 Principles for Surviving and Thriving at Work, Home, and School*. Seattle, WA: Pear Press, 112.

14. Medina, *Brain Rules*, 114.

15. Erikson, E. H. (1982). *The Life Cycle Completed*. New York: W.W. Norton, 72.
16. Gersen, J. S. (2014, December 15). The Trouble with Teaching Rape Law. *New Yorker*. Retrieved from www.newyorker.com/news/news-desk/trouble-teaching-rape-law
17. Lukianoff & Haidt, *The Coddling of the American Mind*, 29.
18. Taleb, N. N. (2012). *Antifragile*. New York: Random House, 3.

Chapter 3

1. American Psychiatric Association. (2013). *Diagnostic and Statistical Manual of Mental Disorders* (5th ed.; *DSM-5*). Washington, DC: American Psychiatric Association, 222.
2. Lack, M. (2013, September 25). *Piglet—A Case Study in Generalized Anxiety Disorder* [Video File]. Posted by Professor Caleb Lack. Retrieved from https://www.youtube.com/watch?v=2eKVCqZsehk
3. American Psychiatric Association, *DSM-5*, 222.
4. Siegel, D. J., & Bryson, T. P. (2012). *The Whole-Brain Child*. New York: Bantam, 27.
5. Smith, M. L., & Glass, G. V. (1977). Meta-Analysis of Psychotherapy Outcome Studies. *American Psychologist*, 32(9), 752–760. http://dx.doi.org/10.1037/0003-066X.32.9.752
6. Lawlis, F. (2008). *Retraining the Brain*. New York: Plume, 30.
7. Hayes, S. C. (2004). Acceptance and Commitment Therapy, Relational Frame Theory, and the Third Wave of Behavioral and Cognitive Therapies. *Behavior Therapy*, 35, 639–665. DOI: 10.1016/S0005-7894(04)80013-3
8. Boggart. Harry Potter Wiki. Retrieved from https://harrypotter.fandom.com/wiki/Boggart

a. Clark, D., & Beck, A. (2012). *The Anxiety and Worry Workbook*. New York: Guilford Press, 18.
b. Clark & Beck, *The Anxiety and Worry Workbook*, 18.

Chapter 4

1. Clark, D., & Beck, A. (2012). *The Anxiety and Worry Workbook*. New York: Guilford Press; Mathews, H. (2014). *Un-agoraphobic*. San Francisco, CA: Weiser Books, x.
2. American Psychiatric Association. (2013). *Diagnostic and Statistical Manual of Mental Disorders* (5th ed.; *DSM-5*). Washington, DC: American Psychiatric Association, 208.
3. Kearney, C. A., Albano, A. M., Eisen, A. R., Allan, W. D., & Barlow, D. H. (1997). The Phenomenology of Panic Disorder in Youngsters: An Empirical Study of a Clinical Sample. *Journal of Anxiety Disorders*, 11, 49–62, 55.
4. "Change of a Dress." (2002). *Sex and the City*, season 4. Written by J. Rottenberg & E. Zuritsky. Directed by A. Taylor. United States: HBO.
5. American Psychiatric Association, *DSM-5*, 208.
6. American Psychiatric Association, *DSM-5*, 208.
7. Mathews, *Un-agoraphobic*, xi–xii.
8. American Psychiatric Association, *DSM-5*, 217.
9. Tompkins, M. A., & Martinez, K. (2010). *My Anxious Mind: A Teen's Guide to Managing Anxiety and Panic*. Washington, DC: Magination Press, 95.

10. Tompkins & Martinez, *My Anxious Mind*, 104.

11. Mathews, *Un-agoraphobic*, 27.

12. Chansky, T. E. (2004). *Freeing Your Child from Anxiety*. New York: Broadway Books, 191.

13. Mathews, *Un-agoraphobic*, 6.

14. Welsh, J. (2011, September 14). Why Laughter May Be the Best Pain Medicine. *Scientific American*. Retrieved from https://www.scientificamerican.com/article/why-laughter-may-be-the-best-pain-medicine/

15. Mathews, *Un-agoraphobic*, x.

a. Beidel, D. C., & Turner, S. M. (2005). *Childhood Anxiety Disorders*. New York: Taylor & Francis, 283

Chapter 5

1. Brodsky, S. (2018, July 11). Personal interview.

2. Tolin, D. (2012). *Face Your Fears: A Proven Plan to Beat Anxiety, Panic, Phobias, and Obsessions*. Hoboken, NJ: John Wiley & Sons, 107.

3. Tolin, *Face Your Fears*, 129.

a. Umbach, A. (2015). *Conquer your Fears and Phobias for Teens: How to Build Courage and Stop Fear from Holding You Back*. Oakland, CA: Instant Help Books, 21.

b. Chansky, T. E. (2004). *Freeing Your Child from Anxiety*. New York: Broadway Books, 144.

Chapter 6

1. Chansky, T. E. (2004). *Freeing Your Child from Anxiety*. New York: Broadway Books, 147.

2. Leary, M. R., & Kowalski, R. M. (1995). *Social Anxiety*. New York: Guilford Press, 32.

Chapter 7

1. Bandelow, B, Michaelis, S., & Wedekind, D. (2017). Treatment of Anxiety Disorders. *Dialogues in Clinical Neuroscience, 19*(2), 93–107.

2. Epictus, translated by George Long. (2004). *The Enchiridion*. New York: Dover, 3.

3. Aurelius, M. (2002). *Meditations*, IV.7. New York: Modern Library, 39.

4. Bandelow, Michaelis, & Wedekind, Treatment of Anxiety Disorders, 93–107.

5. Shedler, J. (2010). The Efficacy of Psychodynamic Psychotherapy. *American Psychologist, 65*(2), 98–109. DOI: 10.1037/a0018378, 98.

6. Shedler, The Efficacy of Psychodynamic Psychotherapy, 98–109.

7. Shedler, The Efficacy of Psychodynamic Psychotherapy, 98–109.

8. Kazdin, A., Marciano, P., & Whitely, M. (2005). The Therapeutic Alliance in Cognitive-Behavioral Treatment of Children Referred for Oppositional, Aggressive and Antisocial Behavior. *Journal of Consulting & Clinical Psychology, 73*(4), 726–730.

9. Lebowitz, E. R., & Omer, H. (2013). *Treating Childhood and Adolescent Anxiety: A Guide for Caregivers*. Hoboken, NJ: John Wiley & Sons, 5.

10. Bandelow, B., Markus, R., Rover, C., Michaelis, S., Gorlich, Y., & Wedekind, D. (2015). Efficacy of Treatments for Anxiety Disorders: A Meta-Analysis. *International Clinical Psychopharmacology, 30*(4), 183–192. DOI: 10.1097/YIS.0000000000000078

11. Medina, J. (2014). *Brain Rules: 12 Principles for Surviving and Thriving at Work, Home, and School.* Seattle, WA: Pear Press, 47.

12. Medina, *Brain Rules,* 24.

13. Medina, *Brain Rules,* 35.

14. Wang, T. W., Grentzke, A., Sharapova, S., Cullen, K. A., Ambrose, B. K., & Jamal, A. (2018). Tobacco Product Use Among Middle and High School Students—United States, 2011–2017. *Morbidity and Mortality Weekly Report, 67,* 629–633. DOI: http://dx.doi.org/10.15585/mmwr.mm6722a3

15. US Department of Health and Human Services. (N.d.). Adolescents and Tobacco: Trends. HHS.gov. Retrieved from https://www.hhs.gov/ash/oah/adolescent-development/substance-use/drugs/tobacco/trends/index.html#_ftn2

16. Johnston, L. D., Miech, R. A., O'Malley, P. M., Bachman, J. G., Schulenberg, J. E., & Patrick, M. E. (2018). *Monitoring the Future National Survey Results on Drug Use: 1975–2017: Overview, Key Findings on Adolescent Drug Use.* Ann Arbor, MI: Institute for Social Research, University of Michigan; Lawrence, D., Considine, J., Mitrou, F., & Zubrick, S. R. (2010). Anxiety Disorders and Cigarette Smoking: Results from the Australian Survey of Mental Health and Wellbeing. *The Australian and New Zealand Journal of Psychiatry, 44*(6), 520–527. doi: 10.3109/00048670903571580

17. Raven, K. (2019, September 7). Teen Vaping Linked to More Health Risks. Yale Medicine. Retrieved from http:www.yalemedicine.org/stories/teen-vaping/; Pedersen, W., & von Soest, T. (2009). Smoking, Nicotine Dependence and Mental Health among Young Adults: A 13-Year Population-Based Longitudinal Study. *Addiction, 104*(1),129–137. DOI: 10.1111/j.1360-0443.2008.02395.x

18. Arain, M., Haque, M., Johal, L., Mathur, P., Nel, W., Rais, A., Sanhu, R., & Sharma, S. (2013). Maturation of the Adolescent Brain. *Neuropsychiatric Disease and Treatment, 9,* 449–461. DOI: 10.2147/NDT.S39776

19. US Department of Health and Human Services. (2017, December 14). Vaping Popular among Teens; Opioid Misuse at Historic Lows. National Institutes of Health. Retrieved from https://www.nih.gov/news-events/news-releases/vaping-popular-among-teens-opioid-misuse-historic-lows

20. US Department of Health and Human Services. (2016). *E-Cigarette Use among Youth and Young Adults: A Report of the Surgeon General.* Rockville, MD: US Department of Health and Human Services. Retrieved from https://www.cdc.gov/tobacco/data_statistics/sgr/e-cigarettes/pdfs/2016_sgr_entire_report_508.pdf

21. Centers for Disease Control and Prevention. (N.d.). About Electronic Cigarettes (E-Cigarettes). CDC.gov. Retrieved from http://www.cdc.gov/tobacco/basic_information/e-cigarettes/about-e-cigarettes.html

22. Barrington-Trimis, J. L., Samet, J. M., & McConnell, R. (2014). Flavorings in Electronic Cigarettes: An Unrecognized Respiratory Health Hazard? *JAMA, 312*(23), 2493–2494. DOI: 10.1001/jama.2014.14830

23. Wegner, D. M., & Schneider, D. J. (1987). Paradoxical Effects of Thought Suppression. *Journal of Personality and Social Psychology, 53*(1), 8.

24. Dostoyevsky, F. (1863). *Winter Notes on Summer Impressions.* Evanston, IL: Northwestern University Press, 49.

25. Goldin, P. R., McRae, K., Ramel, W., & Gross, J. J. (2008). The Neural Bases of Emotion Regulation: Reappraisal and Suppression of Negative Emotion. *Biological Psychiatry, 63*(6), 577–586.

26. Medina, *Brain Rules*, 94.

27. Valk, S., Bernhardt, B., Fynn-Mathis, T., Bockler, A., Kanske, P., Guizard, N., Collins, D., & Singer, T. (2017). Structural Plasticity of the Social Brain: Differential Change after Socio-affective and Cognitive Mental Training. *Science Advances, 3*(10). DOI: 10.1126/sciadv.1700489

28. Gregoire, C. (2017, January 18). Talking to a Therapist Can Literally Rewire Your Brain. *HuffPost*. Retrieved from https://www.huffpost.com/entry/therapy-brain-changes_n_587e440ce4b07b9dd704c13b

Chapter 8

1. American Psychiatric Association, *Diagnostic and Statistical Manual of Mental Disorders* (5th ed.; *DSM-5*). (2013). Washington, DC: American Psychiatric Association, 238.

2. American Psychiatric Association, *DSM-5*, 242.

3. American Psychiatric Association, *DSM-5*, 329.

4. American Psychiatric Association, *DSM-5*, 339.

5. American Psychiatric Association, *DSM-5*, 161.

Chapter 9

1. Lebowitz, E.R., Omer, H., Hermes, H., & Scahill, L. (2014). Parent Training for Childhood Anxiety Disorders: The SPACE Program. *Cognitive and Behavioral Practice, 21*, 457.

2. Lebowitz, E. R., & Omer, H. (2013). *Treating Childhood and Adolescent Anxiety: A Guide for Caregivers*. Hoboken, NJ: John Wiley & Sons, 36–37.

3. Lebowitz, E. R., Woolston, J. W., Bar-Haim, Y., Calvocoressi, L., Dauser, C., Warnick, E., Scahill, L., Chakir, A. R., Chechner, T., Hermes, H., Vitulano, L. A., King, R. A., & Leckman, J. F. (2013). Family Accommodation in Pediatric Anxiety Disorders. *Depression and Anxiety, 30*(1), 47–54. DOI: 10.1002/da.21998.

4. Lebowitz & Omer, *Treating Childhood and Adolescent Anxiety*, 46.

5. Lebowitz, Woolston, et al. Family Accommodation in Pediatric Anxiety Disorders, 47–54.

6. Twenge, J. (2017). *iGen*. New York: Atria Paperback, 154.

7. Twenge, *iGen*, 167.

8. Lukianoff, G., & Haidt, J. (2018). *The Coddling of the American Mind*. New York: Penguin Press, 170.

9. Lebowitz & Omer, *Treating Childhood and Adolescent Anxiety*, 128.

10. @r/Showerthoughts. (2017, July 4). Never in the History of Calming Down Meme. *Reddit*. Retrieved from https://www.reddit.com/r/Showerthoughts/comments/3zbuvl/never_in_the_history_of_calming_down_has_anyone/

11. Medina, J. (2014). *Brain Rules: 12 Principles for Surviving and Thriving at Work, Home, and School*. Seattle, WA: Pear Press, 78.

12. McDonagh, T., & Hatcher, J.P. (2016). *101 Ways to Conquer Teen Anxiety*. Berkeley, CA: Ulysses Press, 3.
13. Lebowitz & Omer, *Treating Childhood and Adolescent Anxiety*, 92.
14. Lebowitz & Omer, *Treating Childhood and Adolescent Anxiety*, 94.
15. Lebowitz & Omer, *Treating Childhood and Adolescent Anxiety*, 155.
16. Lebowitz, Omer, et al. Parent Training for Childhood Anxiety Disorders, 466.
17. Lebowitz, E., Marin, C., Martino, A., Shimshoni, Y., & Silverman, W. (2019). Parent-Based Treatment as Efficacious as Cognitive Behavioral Therapy for Childhood Anxiety: A Randomized Noninferiority Study of Supportive Parenting for Anxious Childhood Emotions. *Journal of the American Academy of Childhood & Adolescent Psychiatry*. DOI: https://doi.org/10.1016/j.jaac.2019.02.014

Conclusion

1. Lebowitz, E. (2018, June 19). Personal interview.
2. Lawlis, F. (2008) *Retraining the Brain*. New York: Plume, 36.
3. Lawlis, *Retraining the Brain*, 32–33.

Further Reading

Books

American Psychiatric Association. (2013). *Diagnostic and Statistical Manual of Mental Disorders* (5th ed.). Washington, DC: American Psychiatric Association.

Beidel, D. C., & Turner, S. M. (2005). *Childhood Anxiety Disorders*. New York: Taylor & Francis.

Chansky, T. E. (2004). *Freeing Your Child from Anxiety*. New York: Broadway Books.

Clark, D., & Beck, A. (2012). *The Anxiety and Worry Workbook*. New York: Guilford Press.

Lawlis, F. (2008). *Retraining the Brain*. New York: Plume.

Leary, M. R., & Kowalski, R. M. (1995). *Social Anxiety*. New York: Guilford Press.

Lebowitz, E. R., & Omer, H. (2013). *Treating Childhood and Adolescent Anxiety: A Guide for Caregivers*. Hoboken, NJ: John Wiley & Sons.

Lukianoff, G., & Haidt, J. (2018). *The Coddling of the American Mind*. New York: Penguin Press.

Mathews, H. (2014). *Un-agoraphobic*. San Francisco, CA: Weiser Books.

McDonagh, T., & Hatcher, J. P. (2016). *101 Ways to Conquer Teen Anxiety*. Berkeley, CA: Ulysses Press.

Medina, J. (2014). *Brain Rules: 12 Principles for Surviving and Thriving at Work, Home, and School*. Seattle, WA: Pear Press.

Taleb, N. N. (2012). *Antifragile*. New York: Random House.

Tolin, D. (2012). *Face Your Fears: A Proven Plan to Beat Anxiety, Panic, Phobias, and Obsessions*. Hoboken, NJ: John Wiley & Sons.

Tompkins, M. A., & Martinez, K. (2010). *My Anxious Mind: A Teen's Guide to Managing Anxiety and Panic*. Washington, DC: Magination Press.

Twenge, J. (2017). *iGen*. New York: Atria Paperback.

Umbach, A. (2015). *Conquer Your Fears and Phobias for Teens: How to Build Courage and Stop Fear from Holding You Back*. Oakland, CA: Instant Help Books.

Articles

Arain, M., Haque, M., Johal, L., Mathur, P., Nel, W., Rais, A., Sanhu, R., & Sharma, S. (2013). Maturation of the Adolescent Brain. *Neuropsychiatric Disease and Treatment, 9*, 449–461. DOI: 10.2147/NDT.S39776

Bandelow, B., Markus, R., Rover, C., Michaelis, S., Gorlich, Y., & Wedekind, D. (2015). Efficacy of Treatments for Anxiety Disorders: A Meta-Analysis. *International Clinical Psychopharmacology, 30*(4), 183–192. DOI: 10.1097/YIS.0000000000000078

Bandelow, B., Michaelis, S., & Wedekind, D. (2017). Treatment of Anxiety Disorders. *Dialogues in Clinical Neuroscience, 19*(2), 93–107.

Goldin, P. R., McRae, K., Ramel, W., & Gross, J. J. (2008). The Neural Bases of Emotion Regulation: Reappraisal and Suppression of Negative Emotion. *Biological Psychiatry, 63*(6), 577–586.

Gregoire, C. (2017, January 18). Talking to a Therapist Can Literally Rewire Your Brain. *HuffPost*. Retrieved from https://www.huffpost.com/entry/therapy-brain-changes_n_587e440ce4b07b9dd704c13b

Kazdin, A., Marciano, P., & Whitely, M. (2005). The Therapeutic Alliance in Cognitive-Behavioral Treatment of Children Referred for Oppositional, Aggressive and Antisocial Behavior. *Journal of Consulting & Clinical Psychology, 73*(4), 726–730.

Kearney, C. A., Albano, A. M., Eisen, A. R., Allan, W. D., & Barlow, D. H. (1997). The Phenomenology of Panic Disorder in Youngsters: An Empirical Study of a Clinical Sample. *Journal of Anxiety Disorders, 11*, 49–62.

Kessler, R. C., Chiu, W. T., Demler, O., Merikangas, K. R., & Walters, E. E. (2005). Prevalence, Severity, and Comorbidity of 12-Month *DSM-IV* Disorders in the National Comorbidity Survey Replication. *Archives of General Psychiatry, 62*(6), 617–627. PMID: 15939839

Lebowitz, E., Marin, C., Martino, A., Shimshoni, Y., & Silverman, W. (2019). Parent-Based Treatment as Efficacious as Cognitive Behavioral Therapy for Childhood Anxiety: A Randomized Noninferioriity Study of Supportive Parenting for Anxious Childhood Emotions. *Journal of the American Academy of Childhood & Adolescent Psychiatry*. DOI: https://doi.org/10.1016/j.jaac.2019.02.014

Lebowitz, E. R., Omer, H., Hermes, H., & Scahill, L. (2014). Parent Training for Childhood Anxiety Disorders: The SPACE Program. *Cognitive and Behavioral Practice, 21*, 456–469.

Lebowitz, E. R., Woolston, J. W., Bar-Haim, Y., Calvocoressi, L., Dauser, C., Warnick, E., Scahill, L., Chakir, A. R., Chechner, T., Hermes, H., Vitulano, L. A., King, R. A., & Leckman, J. F. (2013). Family Accommodation in Pediatric Anxiety Disorders. *Depression and Anxiety, 30*(1), 47–54. DOI: 10.1002/da.21998

Shedler, J. (2010). The Efficacy of Psychodynamic Psychotherapy. *American Psychologist, 65*(2), 98–109. DOI: 10.1037/a0018378

Smith, M. L., & Glass, G. V. (1977). Meta-Analysis of Psychotherapy Outcome Studies. *American Psychologist, 32*(9), 752–760. http://dx.doi.org/10.1037/0003-066X.32.9.752

Valk, S., Bernhardt, B., Fynn-Mathis, T., Bockler, A., Kanske, P., Guizard, N., Collins, D., & Singer T. (2017). Structural Plasticity of the Social Brain: Differential Change after Socio-Affective and Cognitive Mental Training. *Science Advances, 3*(10). DOI: 10.1126/sciadv.1700489

Wegner, D. M., Schneider, D. J., Carter, S. R., & White, T. L. (1987). Paradoxical Effects of Thought Suppression. *Journal of Personality and Social Psychology, 53*(1), 5–13.

Index

academics, 22–23, 42, 148, 154

adrenaline, 3–5, 18, 77

agoraphobia: causes, 60; definition and symptoms, 60; treatment, 62–68

aromatherapy, 67

avoidance, 18–19, 34–35, 41, 58, 60, 62, 71, 81–82, 85, 93, 109, 112, 128, 146

benzodiazepines, 65, 84, 95, 114

black-and-white thinking, 11, 15, 148

catastrophizing, 2, 10–11, 15

cognitive distortions, 5–15, 18, 74, 103

cognitive restructuring, 80–81, 83, 103–104, 112

control, need for, 7–8

crisis. See intensive therapy

cyberbullying, 25

deep breathing, 52, 67, 104

depression. See major depressive disorder

eating disorders, 116–117, 118, 125, 128–133, 139, 140; anorexia nervosa, 129; bulimia, 129, 132

emotional reasoning, 11–12

Erikson, Erik, 32

exercise, 52, 53–54, 66–67, 117–118

exposure hierarchy, 78–80, 89

exposure therapy, 64, 77–80, 82, 88–89, 91, 95, 97

fight-or-flight response, 3–4, 18, 116

friendship, 23–24, 27–28, 38, 42–43

generalized anxiety disorder: causes, 40; comorbidity, 125–127; definition and symptoms, 37–39; treatment, 44–53, 104

genetics, 40, 59, 60, 73, 157

grounding technique, 67

hierarchy of fears. See exposure hierarchy

humor, 52–53, 67

imaginal exposure, 79

intensive therapy, 109, 112–113

intolerance: of anxiety, 14–15; of uncertainty, 2, 6–7

labeling, 13–14

mammalian diving reflex, 67

major depressive disorder, 41, 53, 58, 61, 68, 112, 118, 125, 130–131, 133–137, 140–141, 158

mantra, 53, 54

medical concerns. See physical conditions

medication, 41, 45–47, 53, 64–65, 82–84, 94–95, 97, 111–115, 128, 131, 135–136, 139, 140, 159

mind reading, 9–10, 18, 148

mindfulness, 50–51, 122–123

motivation, 97–99, 108–109, 163

negative filtering, 12–13

news, 29–31

nutrition, 116–117

obsessive-compulsive disorder, 82, 103, 110, 126–128

panic attacks, 55–68

panic disorder: causes 59; definition and symptoms, 58; treatment, 62–68

parents, 22, 31–32, 86, 97, 109, 143–162

performance anxiety, 95–99

physical conditions, 66, 120–121
posttraumatic stress disorder, 34, 88, 128, 130
probability overestimation, 9, 74, 103
psychodynamic psychotherapy, 89–90, 97, 105–107
psychoeducation, 108, 112

safety behaviors, 34, 81–82, 93, 127
safety-ism, 33–35, 150–151
screen time, 23–25, 158
self-help books, 51, 65, 92
self-talk, 83, 90–91, 94
sleep, 115–116
smoking, 118–119, 134

social anxiety: definition and symptoms, 85–88; examples of, 111, 130; treatment, 88–95, 103
social media, 23–30, 32, 42, 158
social phobia. *See* social anxiety
specific phobias: causes, 73–74; definition and symptoms, 71–73; treatment, 77–84
substance use, 117, 132–136
SSRI and SNRI, 45–46, 64, 82–84, 94–95, 111, 114
sympathetic nervous system, 3–4

therapeutic alliance, 107–108

vaping and juuling, 119–120

About the Author

Kate Frommer Cik is a psychologist who has worked with children and teenagers in a variety of settings—schools, community mental health centers, and private practice. She graduated magna cum laude from the University of Pennsylvania. She received a master's degree in school psychology and a doctoral degree in child clinical psychology from Yeshiva University. She lives with her husband and three children in Stamford, Connecticut.